Praise for *The First Epistle of Peter: Hope for the 21st Century Man Living in Two Kingdoms*

"Marcus Johnson does an excellent job helping readers gain a thoughtful, down-to-earth understanding of the first letter written by the apostle Peter. He brilliantly connects the dots between Peter's teaching and encouragement to the early Christians with a well-rounded view of Scripture. He also sets the stage well by introducing readers to who Peter was and giving insight into the era in which this epistle was written. I highly recommend reading this book if you want to gain an in-depth understanding of this New Testament letter designed to encourage and challenge its readers for all time."

- ***Chris McClure**, Ordained Pastor, Executive Leadership Coach, and Author of "The Way To Greatness" and "The Magnetic Leader"*

"The Epistle of First Peter: Hope for the 21st Century Man Living in Two Kingdoms is an accessible, useful commentary that will enhance your study of Peter's first letter. It brings Peter's wisdom into the twenty-first century and applies it directly to issues faced in today's world, particularly the issue of suffering. I found it to be easily readable and relatable. It will be a good addition to your library!"

- ***Grace S. Grose**, author of the Quantum Spacewalker series*

Marcus Johnson has captured the heart of what Peter was implanting in the believers of his day. Christians were suffering increasing persecution and struggling. Peter, who is also known as the Apostle of Hope, encouraged those who were facing such torment to look to the hope that was birth in them through the death, burial and resurrection of Christ Jesus and stand in the grace provided by God. Peter had experience much of the same things these believers were and had also incurred much loss. Marcus clearly opens to us the principals Peter was sowing among the children of God who were under persecution throughout the region. Looking to what lays before the Body of Christ today, the words held within these pages can be a source of strength and encouragement to all believers. The profound simplicity of the commentary held in these pages will make this book a welcome addition to any library.

- **Richard M. Hatfield** – *Pastor and teacher. Founder of Healing Touch of Love Ministries, Author of Hope Brings Life.*

The First Epistle of Peter

Biblical Commentary

HOPE FOR THE 21ST CENTURY MAN LIVING IN TWO KINGDOMS

Marcus Johnson

Also By Marcus Johnson

My Personal Desert Storm: Eating Crow and Humble Pie
(2020 Author Elite Award Winner – Best Memoir)

Breaking Free From the Shadows
(Book 1 of The Wilderness Project)

The First Epistle of Peter

Biblical Commentary

HOPE FOR THE 21ST CENTURY MAN LIVING IN TWO KINGDOMS

Marcus Johnson

The Wilderness
Project Experience

Visit Marcus's website: www.thewildernessprojectexperience.com
The Book of First Peter: Hope for the 21st Century man living in two Kingdoms
The Wilderness Project Experience – Marcus Johnson

Copyright @ 2021 Marcus Johnson

Publish Location: Clermont, Florida

First Edition published 2021

Series: First Peter: Hope for the 21st Century Man

ISBN: 979-8-51965-174-5

ISBN (hardcover): 978-0-57893-490-7

Library of Congress Control Number: 2021912881

This Biblical Commentary book has a companion Workbook of the same title that is sold separately.

Additional information and background about "The First Epistle of Peter: Hope for the 21st Century Man Living in Two Kingdoms", can be found at the website below.

thewildernessprojectexperience.com/

1 Peter 4:19

"So then, those who suffer according to God's will, should commit themselves to their faithful Creator and continue to do good."

Table of Contents

Introduction

Circa 63 AD, scattered throughout Pontus, Galatia, Cappadocia, Asia Minor, and Bithynia, were Christian converts experiencing undefined degrees of suffering and persecution, most likely at the hands of pagans and unbelievers. Located in what is now modern-day Turkey, these Christian communities were living under the rule of the Roman Emperor Nero, who was in the initial stages of a campaign that would soon come to terrorize "Christ followers." There is little doubt that the culture in which Christians were living was highly resistant to their belief system, with slander and ridicule likely increasing at an exponential rate.

At some point, the Apostle Peter, who was most likely residing in Rome at the time, had received news of what these Christians were enduring. He was compelled to write to them, admonishing them to remember the grace and peace that is found in Jesus Christ and the reason they had converted to Christianity in the first place. He was reminding them of the eternal inheritance that awaited them, an inheritance that was imperishable and could not be taken away, no matter what – so he exhorted them to remain steadfast in their faith and confident of who they were in Christ.

For more than thirty years Peter had been serving as one of the Chief Apostles in the Church, traveling, evangelizing, ministering, and planting Churches in areas reaching from the Middle East to Turkey to Rome, and everywhere in between. Over these three decades, it is certain that he saw a lot, experienced much, and learned a great deal. At Pentecost, which we read about in chapter 2 in the Book of Acts, Peter was one of the witnesses that experienced the fire of the baptism in the Holy Spirit, and addressed the crowd, immediately bringing 3000 people to Christ as a result.

However, none of that could compare to what he had personally experienced while walking with Jesus for three years, watching Him being beaten before being crucified, and speaking with Jesus after His resurrection. All of his experiences and all that he had personally witnessed were compounded by revelation after revelation that he received from Christ via the Holy Spirit. What Peter shared with the Christians in Turkey around 63 AD would encapsulate everything he had learned since the moment Jesus gave him the command "Follow Me!". Christ followers today, 21st Century men, are blessed to have the opportunity to mentally consume and heartfully digest the teachings of Peter to this very day.

Peter would tell suffering Christians, the exiled elect of God, that there is a living Hope even in the midst of their suffering. Peter recognized the paradox of rejoicing while suffering; but his letter was real and raw, reminding his readers that they must continue to follow the pattern of conduct set by Christ, for the suffering that Christians experience pales in comparison to the suffering He endured and the glory set before Him. It is this hope in Christ that allowed Christians to persevere in the reality of living their lives following what was then known simply as "The Way."

Peter is honest and transparent, speaking the truth about the persecution, suffering, and the fiery ordeals that Christians will experience. They are told to expect suffering through persecution while simultaneously rejoicing in it and being prepared to give a response when asked by anyone to share, how and why it is possible that they still have hope. The beauty of this teaching, as with all scripture, is that even though Peter wrote it almost 2000 years ago, it parallels events today and, in fact, applies even more to the 21st Century man.

Here, you will find that I will use the words "letter," "epistle," and "book" interchangeably when describing Peter's letter – they are all the same thing, depending on your point of reference. The epistle is first and foremost a letter, which was later canonized in the Bible as a Book, and is often referred to as either "First Book of Peter," or "First Epistle of Peter," depending on the translation used.

As I was initially completing my study of First Peter in preparation for a live video series, I opted to bounce back and forth between three main translations (NASB, ESV, and CSB). I was interested not only in what Peter had to say, but in how different translations interpret Peter's teachings. This made for an interesting comparison between my study bibles and a Concordance as I wanted to ensure I was interpreting the scripture as accurately as possible. Later, when I decided to take my video series notes and use them as source material for this book, my pursuits led me to expand the number of different bible translations for each section of Peter's letter, ultimately settling on thirteen carefully selected versions, from literal to freer translations that bring out certain meanings in the modern context, which will no doubt help the reader gain further insight into biblical truths.

At the beginning of each chapter in this book, I label the translation used for scripture in that chapter, but you can also find a list of every translation used at the end of this book, along with descriptions of each translation for those that you may not be familiar with. I would encourage you to have your own favorite bible handy as you read this book so that you can cross reference it with the translations used in each chapter and complete your own parallel assessment. Nonetheless, none of this detracts from the commentary or ensuing discussion of that section of Peter's letter.

What I thoroughly enjoy about detailed Book studies, verses a topical study, is the opportunity to learn more about the author of those letters, at an intimate level, based on the Spirit-led context of the letter he wrote. Secondly, it offers a doorway into learning more about the people of the time the letter was written to, to learn more about the participants in the stories shared, to fully understand the integrity and authoritative context of why the letter was written, and why the author wrote the letter in the first place (it's true theme and purpose). More often than not, when we as Christians are meditating and digesting God's Word, we pull and extract verses from different areas of Scripture that enlighten us on a specific topic, event, or area of our life, or the life of a loved one. As people of God, this type of meditative study is important to our faith as it enriches our spirit and must be done as the Holy Spirit guides.

> *1 Peter 2:10: "Once you were not a people, but now you are the people of God…"*

However, we also hear of, or correctly judge for ourselves, instances of how scriptures are taken out of context and used to incorrectly fit into or justify a believer's particular bent – and this can get us into trouble. This is usually due to three things: 1) we fail to consider scripture based on the background, who, and why the letter was originally written; 2) we fail to accurately interpret some of the words in the verse based on the original Greek or Hebrew; or 3) we fail to accurately contextualize the verse based on the verses that preceded and/or followed it. The best way to overcome this is to take time to study the Word on your own and stop depending solely on Sunday morning services. I would also advise you, the 21st Century man, not to depend on this book alone to tell you everything about Peter's First Book. Study it for yourself. You may find some additional areas of enlightenment that I don't as well as areas where we may have disagreement.

> *2 Timothy 2:15 (NKJV): "Be diligent to present yourself approved to God...rightly dividing the word of truth."*

I chose to write about the First Book of Peter for two reasons: 1) Peter is my favorite Disciple/Apostle, which I share about in Chapter 1, and 2) I knew that completing a detailed video series (which later served as the source for this book) would be a complex project, so I wanted to focus on one of the shorter Books from the New Testament. Viola, the First Book of Peter it was!

What I did not expect was the challenging depth of my own character development that I would be undertaking. I took this study seriously, not just for the audience I would be speaking to on a weekly basis, but for myself. What would God reveal to me, personally and spiritually, as I dedicated my time to this project? It took me 24 weeks to complete that video series – every week – and I was not disappointed (why would I be?).

For this study, I needed to address two questions during each of the 24 videos and for all fourteen sections of this book: 1) How did each verse apply to the specific people that Peter was writing to at the time, and 2) How can I, a 21st Century man, apply Peter's teachings to my life without violating the integrity of the letter? As I studied each passage, I allowed the Holy Spirit to guide the interpretive commentary I was developing, but I also went back to the commentary of my three study bibles to test, confirm, or rebuff my own interpretations.

Much of Peter's letter is based on suffering and, if we aren't observant enough, we can easily miss the spiritual and teachable nuggets of HOPEFUL wisdom and grace contained within. The task may seem daunting, but I can't over-emphasize the amount of growth I personally experienced as a result. God's grace is amazing, the most wonderful experience one can have. Sometimes the truth can be hard to digest, and the truth revealed in Peter's First Letter does not hold back hard truths about faith, grace, salvation, and submission. Let me be clear about this letter: Peter is real, and he is raw, and some of the truths he shares may sting a bit. I know it did for me as I surveyed my own character and behavior based on his teachings.

> *1 Peter 2:13: "Submit yourself for the Lord's sake to every human authority: whether to the emperor, as the supreme authority..."*

6

Introduction

May this commentary bless you with the challenging thoughts and ideas that Peter teaches from his letter! May the eyes and ears of your heart be opened to something new, something that you had not seen before, to enlighten and encourage you in your own walk with Christ! As you come across the challenging passages, particularly in the area of submission, may the mind of your heart be opened to revealing shortcomings or lapses in your own Christian character from which you can grow! If you have never before studied Peter's letter from beginning to end, it will test you and force you to assess your own faith for hidden areas of pride. But, more importantly, this letter will give you HOPE in a time that it is needed more than ever. May this book offer you the same degree of HOPE it did for me, as a 21st Century man, while living in two Kingdoms! God bless.

1 Peter 5:14 (NASB): "Greet one another with a kiss of love. Peace be to you all who are in Christ."

1

Who Was the Apostle Peter?

I believe that to properly understand the First Book of Peter, we ought to know a little about the man who is credited with writing it – at least have a cursory examination of who he was. This is not a book about Peter, so we won't spend a lot of time here; but we need to know a little about who he was in order to understand why he takes the positions he does within his first book. As I began my research into the man, the amount of information was overwhelming, which by itself, says a lot about Peter. Unfortunately, doctrine and tradition have overshadowed who Peter really was, and this has caused some controversy within the body.

Peter is my favorite disciple of the original twelve disciples of Jesus Christ, which is one of the reasons I was compelled to complete my own intimate study of Peter's First Book. I like him because I can relate to him; he is real and authentic to me, full of contradictions. He was arrogant and he was pompous, he had courage and was not afraid of confrontation. He was bold, he was spontaneous; but he was also cowardly and he was a very flawed man, which was obvious to those who knew him. But Jesus also saw something in Peter that was strong, reliable, and dependable, so much so that He personally invited Peter to be part of His inner circle of three (in addition to James and John). Jesus referred to Peter as the "rock" (*Cephas*), the foundation on which His church would be built (John 1:42).

More importantly, Peter, flaws and all, was a leader. I believe it was exactly because of his flaws that the Lord discipled him in order to make him a leader of men in His Church. Why? Because Peter would be working to minister and save men who were just like him. After Jesus was resurrected and ascended to heaven, Peter became one of the most influential Christian leaders of the Christian movement and is always listed first among the twelve disciples in the gospels.

One of his counterparts, the Apostle Paul, typically gets more attention and fame than Peter, as the preponderance of books of the New Testament credited to Paul show. But Peter was a personal eyewitness to Jesus on earth whereas Paul was not. Peter walked with Jesus, Peter spoke with Jesus, Peter prayed with Jesus, and Peter was the only Disciple to actually walk on water (a few steps anyway). Peter defended Jesus and cut off a soldier's ear when He was being arrested while the others ran off in fear. But Peter also later denied knowing Jesus – and his denial broke him. However, it was Peter's brokenness that ultimately allowed God to restore him to a position of glory and honor, raising him to be the pillar of the church that he was destined to be. It was Peter that addressed the large crowds at Pentecost, and as we are told in Acts 2:14-41, over 3000 people converted to Christianity that day.

We know a lot about Peter based on what is shared in Scripture, but he was also prominent and popular enough in his time for historians and church leaders of his era and afterwards to write extensively about him. This allows us to have a further glimpse into who Peter was beyond Scripture.

Though the gospels vary on the specifics about the first meeting between Peter and Jesus, it is clear that Peter was a fisherman by trade when Jesus called out to him and said, "Follow Me!", along with his brother Andrew. It is interesting that the three disciples (Peter, James, and John) who were Jesus' inner circle, were all fishermen. Peter was married, as alluded to in the Books of Matthew, Mark and Luke, as well as briefly mentioned by Paul in 1 Corinthians 9:5, but Peter's brother is the only family member we regularly see in scripture.

The gospels draw a picture of Peter being impulsive and rash, never afraid to speak his mind. But, as we find in the Book of Acts, it was Peter's character and his ability to make quick and effective decisions that marked him as someone who was dependable and who everyone could turn to. Peter was disciplined. Perhaps it was because of Jesus' foreknowledge of who Peter would become that he referred to Peter as "the rock" on whom Jesus would build His church (Matthew 16:17-18). It is also fair to note that Jesus made this statement after Peter was the first to identify Jesus as the promised Messiah. Either way, Peter's leadership is obvious.

The Book of Acts shows us that the early church relied heavily on Peter, but James (Jesus' brother) and John were relied on as well. It was these three that primarily made decisions as the early church developed its doctrinal and organizational structure. While Peter was focused predominantly on ministering to the Jews, he was the first person to experience a vision from God in reference to how the Gentiles fit into God's plan; nonetheless, it was Apostle Paul who was called out to minister directly to the Gentiles.

While James (Jesus' brother) became the de facto head of the Church from Jerusalem, Paul would depend on Peter as one of the three heads to influence James and John regarding decisions when it came to how Gentiles would be integrated in regard to doctrine within the church.[1] As Paul held the dominant influence over the Gentiles, he was concerned that if Peter, James, or John could not support what Paul was already preaching to the Gentiles, then why would the Galatians accept anything that Paul, Peter, James, or John had to say? Thus Peter was the key influencer that Paul needed.

> *"But on the contrary, seeing that I had been entrusted with the gospel to the uncircumcised, just as Peter had been to the circumcised (for He who was at work for Peter in his apostleship to the circumcised was at work for me also to the Gentiles), and recognizing the grace that had been given to me, James and Cephas [**Peter**] and John, who were reputed to be pillars, gave to me and Barnabas the right hand of fellowship, so that we might go to the Gentiles, and they to the circumcised" (Galatians 2:7-9, **Peter's name added for clarity**).*

Again, Peter was one of three disciples to personally witness a side of Jesus that none of the other disciples saw: the first time Jesus resurrected someone from the dead, the moment Jesus revealed who He truly is, and Jesus' most personal and distressing moment.

- Mark 5:35-43: Jesus raises a girl from the dead
- Matthew 17:1-13: the moment when Jesus was transfigured, revealing His divinity
- Matthew 26:36-46: Jesus' desperate prayer to the Father in the Garden of Gethsemane

One of the things that I highly respect about Peter is that he was the one who was never afraid to do, or say, what others were thinking but were either afraid to say or do. But Peter also found himself in the middle of things that I strongly suspect he would have preferred not to be in such a high role:

- Matthew 14:28-33: Peter walks on water.
- Matthew 17:13-20: Peter declares Jesus as the Messiah.
- Luke 22:54-62: Peter denies knowing Jesus three times.
- John 21:15-17: Jesus reinstates Peter and affirms his position as the leader of the Christian movement.
- Acts 2:14-41: Peter addresses the crowd at Pentecost.
- Acts 10:9-48: Peter imparts his vision from God about the Gospel also being for the Gentiles.
- Acts 12:1-19: Peter escapes from prison with the aid of an angel.
- Galatians 2:11-21: Peter is subjected to a confrontation with Paul.

One of the items of debate about Peter is whether or not he truly authored either of the two Epistles with his name and his level of involvement with the Gospel of Mark, given the text found within.[2] I will touch more deeply on the debate about the two Epistles in the next chapter titled "The Book of First Peter," but in this chapter, I will dabble a little into it, as well as the controversy around his participation in writing the Gospel of Mark.

In Acts Chapter 4, we read that Peter was uneducated, which may seem to make it unlikely that Peter wrote either of the two letters with his name. This claim is used by some scholars to discredit the authorship of both books.

> *"Now as they observed the confidence of Peter and John and understood that they were uneducated and untrained men, they were amazed, and began to recognize them as having been with Jesus" (Acts 4:13).*

However, as we will learn in chapter 5 of 1 Peter, Peter most likely dictated his letter to Silas (aka Silvanus) who actually penned the letter.

> *"Through Silvanus, our faithful brother (for so I regard him), I have written to you briefly, exhorting and testifying that this is the true grace of God. Stand firm in it!" (1 Peter 5:12)*

Secondly, First and Second Peter were most likely written between the years 60-64 AD,[3] a time span of approximately 25 years since the comment describing Peter in Acts 4:13. Though there is no mention of it, this would have been plenty of time for Peter to have learned how to read and write, a skill Peter would have desired in support of his ministry efforts. But this is, admittedly, conjecture on my part.

Finally, regarding the Gospel of Mark, while no scholars or theologians posit that Peter wrote any of the parts of the Gospel, it has been argued that Mark wrote the letter based on the personal

14

experiences shared with him from Peter.[4] The Gospel does appear to be written from the awareness and perspective of Peter and Peter is mentioned in every major story found within Mark, so this makes the argument plausible.

However, the Gospel of Mark does not mention a connection between Mark and Peter, which is odd if Peter were the key contributor to the Gospel. Nevertheless, there are two verses in Scripture that do mention a connection between Peter and Mark. The first is found in Acts 12:12 where, after Peter escapes from prison, he remains at Mark's house. The second is found in 1 Peter 5:13 where Mark is included in the closing salutations from Peter to his readers. Note: there is debate if the Mark found in 1 Peter is the same Mark from the Gospel, such is the mystery of the era.

Earlier in this chapter, I alluded to the idea that we know of Peter not just from scripture, but also from the writings of historians and early church leaders. One of those early historians is Eusebius – oh, how I would love to write a book, or at least an interesting blog, about Eusebius at some point! Either way, Eusebius of Caesarea wrote of an account that traces Peter to the Gospel of Mark.

Eusebius (b. 260-265, d. 339-340) was a fourth century historian who is often referred to as the "Father of Church History."[5] He was NOT a church father and was, in fact, excommunicated from the church for heresy, but his writings still have a place in early Christian writings. Eusebius is from the same location, Caesarea, mentioned in the Book of Acts, so he would have had access to thousands of documents from the early church (which have sadly now been destroyed); but many of Eusebius writings have survived.

Eusebius, because of his access to ancient documents of the time, claims to have found documents written by Papias of Hierapolis (a church father who lived c. 60-130 AD) that outlined a personal discussion he had with John the Elder (presumably John the Apostle), who told him that Mark did write the Gospel of Mark based on Peter's personal testimony. I suppose this is a fuzzy "he said" situation, so take that for what you will. Eusebius, coincidentally, is also one of the primary sources of the account of Peter's martyrdom, which occurred around 64 AD.

In John 21:18, Jesus told Peter, *"...when you grow old, you will stretch out your hands and someone else will put your belt on you, and bring you where you do not want to go."* John continues in John 21:19, *"Now He said this, indicating by what kind of death he would glorify God..."* Eusebius quotes from Origen, who was himself a scholar from the 2nd and 3rd centuries, as follows, "Peter was crucified at Rome with his head downwards, as he himself had desired to suffer." But the first, hence oldest, documented record of Peter being crucified upside down is found in a text, known as an apocryphal text, titled *Acts of Peter.*

Flavius Josephus,[6] a Jewish historian from the 1st Century who also claimed Roman citizenship, wrote in his document titled *Jewish War* that Romans did not always crucify people head up as Jesus is depicted in the crucifixion, but that they would occasionally crucify people in different positions as a form of entertainment. Church tradition holds that Peter was crucified upside down around 64 AD after the Great Fire of Rome blamed on Christians by Emperor Nero. Adding to these accounts is a long-held belief that Peter was crucified upside down by his own request as he did not feel worthy to be crucified the same way as Jesus Christ. Some may think that Peter's request was overly "spiritual," but what I see is a man of faithful conviction and an example of true biblical courage.

2

The Book of First Peter (aka, The First Epistle of Peter)

<u>Authorship & Background</u>

If we read, understand, but more importantly believe, that all Scripture is truth, then there can be no doubt that Peter wrote what is known as his First Epistle as affirmed in the very first verse *"Peter, an Apostle to Jesus Christ."* Additionally, 1 Peter 5:1 claims that the author was an *"eyewitness of the sufferings of Christ,"* further affirming Peter's authorship. Nonetheless, there are those that still question and dispute his authorship as mentioned in the previous chapter.

Why is the authorship important and necessary to this discussion? Because, if we can doubt the authorship of the letter, it creates a credibility challenge in regard to the message of the letter itself. Sure, there are some good moral principles of Christian conduct in the letter, but part of the basis of truth is Peter's personal witness and the leadership focus for Elders within. Additionally, if Peter's authorship comes into question, it's a downward slope towards doubts about other books of the Bible, if not the complete Bible itself.

The Book, as authored by Peter, would have been written during the reign of Nero (54-68 AD), most likely between 60-63 AD[1] as Peter is believed to have been crucified in 64 AD[2] as discussed in the previous chapter. Some believe that the Book was written during the reigns of Domitian (81-96 AD) or Trajan (98-117 AD)[3], though I personally could not find sufficient information to support those arguments to my satisfaction. If true, then this would add to the credibility problem for the letter, if not about Peter himself since his death and martyrdom is documented as occurring around 64 AD. To be honest, I did complete some basic research, which I include below, but I did not spend a lot of time striving to collaborate this one way or the other as I believe it would have been a distraction, and since I hold all scripture to be truth, I believe in my heart that this Book was written, or at least dictated, by Peter.

As mentioned in the previous chapter, Acts chapter 4 indicates that Peter was not an educated man and it is plausible he did not personally write this letter. According to scholars that question Peter's authorship:[4]

1) The Greek used in the original text was too sophisticated, something that is claimed a Galilean fisherman would not have used.
2) The theology is much closer to Paul's.

3) Some believe that the background of the letter is more reflective of the Roman emperors Domitian or Trajan, who reigned after Peter's death.

4) It is thought that Peter would have referenced more about Jesus as he was a personal friend of Jesus while He walked the earth.

As for the first two arguments, I previously noted that at least 25 years had lapsed since the description of Peter depicted in Acts 4:13. I have no basis to support my argument, but it is very possible that Peter would have learned to read, write, and comprehend Greek over that 25-year period since Peter would have been highly motivated to learn in an effort to improve his own abilities to support his ministry and the church at large. Additionally, evidence suggests that Silvanus may have actually penned the letter per Peter's dictation.

> *"By Silvanus, our faithful brother (as I consider him), I have written to you briefly, to counsel and testify that this is the true grace [the undeserved favor] of God…"*
> *(1 Peter 5:12, AMP)*

Finally, while they both might have been in competition at times, Paul and Peter were both intent on initiating the Gentiles into the church; therefore their theologies would have meshed, though there is an admitted gap in this thinking, which I will allude to in a bit. Additionally, Silvanus spent time with Paul and would have been familiar with his theology, which may have influenced portions of Peter's letter.

As for the third argument, I am not sure where scholars see an overlap of the language in the letter to the reigns of Emperors that came after Nero. There is a reference to Babylon in Peter's letter, but this is a typical reference to Rome used in the New Testament by Jews predominantly. Otherwise, there is no reference to a specific event or action that can point to a specific point in time that allows us to determine who the reigning Emperor was at the time the letter was written.

Finally, the fourth argument is one that might have some basis in truth, but even it is lackluster at best. Unlike Paul, Peter walked side by side with Jesus for three years, Peter was a part of Jesus' inner circle, and Peter watched as Jesus was beaten and later crucified. Additionally, Jesus personally spoke with Peter after His resurrection, something that would have been profound in Peter's life and likely never forgotten. With these in mind, it may seem surprising that Peter did not include within the Book more details about Jesus that were more intimate and personal. Therefore, I offer the following arguments:

- There are other books, known as apocryphal books, believed to have been authored by Peter that are not included as part of the Bible. There are stories shared within these writings that are more detailed about the life and experiences of Peter.

- It is likely that there are writings that Peter completed prior to First Peter that have since been lost to history. It is highly unlikely that First Peter, written 30 years after Christ was crucified, was the first letter that Peter ever wrote. He may very well have written more intimately about Jesus in these other letters and believed that his readers were familiar with them; but this is admittedly pure conjecture on my part as Peter does not make any reference to previous writings in First Peter.

- Peter was writing this Letter for a specific purpose and Peter may have felt that more intimate references to Jesus would have detracted from that purpose. While Jesus retains Godhead over His Church, He handed responsibility of the Church over to Peter, who took that responsibility seriously.

Theme & Purpose

First Peter was written, and intended, to strengthen and encourage suffering believers who were living in what is today, modern Turkey, and who were apparently facing intense persecution in various forms.[5] There is some debate as to whether this Letter was written at a time when Nero had initiated his policy of aggression towards Christians (around 64 AD) but I fall into the camp that believes it was written just prior to Nero's reign of terror against Christ followers. Nonetheless, it is very likely that Peter knew the direction his world was heading based on the social climate and words of knowledge from the Holy Spirit, as his Letter appears to be – to me anyway – more about preparation and expectation than current aggression.

For the twenty first century man, depending on your prophetic take, at the time of writing of this book in March 2021, our world appears to be heading in a direction that is spinning out of control, giving a "feeling" that persecution against Christian beliefs is imminent. Of course, none of us truly knows what tomorrow will bring in the world, but one thing Christ's followers can be assured of is that we have an inheritance awaiting us, one way or another, in eternity. And this right here is at the core of Peter's Letter and the reason he felt compelled to write a letter to followers exhorting them to endure during their time of suffering.

But the truth is, for men in particular, we don't like to envision what is coming, but when we do we want to do something about it; we want to do something to either prevent it or mitigate the impact of the storm that is certainly coming. Our human nature tends to be fearful, and thoughts about suffering, particularly after living for so long in comfort and peace, have our attention – so we prepare. The question is: what are you preparing for, what are you preparing with, and are you preparing in a way that glorifies God mindful of the grace that He has bestowed upon each of us? We want to feel safe, we want to protect our loved ones, but our focus ought to be on what God's promises are, not on our human responses.

Peter tells us to expect suffering, and that it will happen whether we want it to or not. Peter is real and upfront in this letter as he admonishes his readers to prepare "in expectation" of persecution. We might be in a new season of preparation and expectation today, but what exactly are we supposed to do about it? How are we supposed to react and how are we to conduct ourselves? One obvious area is to guard our hearts and stay the course...with God.

First Peter contains substantial language about suffering and persecution, specifically targeted at an audience that lived two thousand years ago in a geographical location within the boundaries of an occupied territory of the Roman Empire. The people of the time were experiencing some ongoing form of persecution and they were suffering as a result, though Peter is not specific about what this persecution was or what degree of suffering they might be experiencing. Peter advises them about their Christian character and behavior during suffering, but also spends some attention on what is yet to come. As a result, we today must rely on our imaginations to draw a picture of what the people of this time were going through. The pictures you draw will be based on your understanding of history, your understanding of the region, and your personal biases and belief system. You will then naturally compare what you believe these people were going through to what you are personally experiencing today. You can't help it; you just do.

As a Christ follower, when you draw a picture of suffering and persecution in your mind, as it relates to you today, what do you see? Keep that picture, don't lose it. Now, draw a picture of the suffering and persecution you believe is happening in less developed nations today, or, in nations that are hostile to Christianity, such as China, the Middle East, or the northern half of Africa. Now, compare the picture of your suffering with the sufferings of people in those other nations. Do you notice a difference? If you live in a developed nation (typically referred to as a Western nation), how does your persecution compare to a Christian living in China, Syria or Nigeria?

Sometimes, we mistake inconveniences in our lives with suffering, or we feel persecuted when we suddenly feel threatened even when actions have not been taken against us personally (yet).

This is acting in fear verses actual persecution. As Americans or Westerners, we find ourselves in a position where a lifestyle that we have become accustomed to or comfortable with over the last 50-60 years, is suddenly being threatened – at least it feels that way – and this makes us angry while asking "Why are you persecuting me?" Meanwhile, people in China are being arrested and sent to prison for worshipping the Lord in the privacy of their homes or Arab Christians are being pulled from their houses and taken to a ditch where they are shot in the head or beheaded because of their faith. Suffering and persecution is in the eye of the beholder based on their background and experiences. This is something we ought to keep in perspective as we read Peter's Letter regarding our own expectations, and how we are to prepare, when it comes to our time of real suffering and persecution.

Peter's Letter is encouraging faithfulness while under oppression, but more specifically, Peter is emphasizing that suffering is normal and expected for believers because we are temporary residents in this world. We want HOPE in a world that is not our forever home, but yet, we may feel we lack rights and should not expect to receive justice in this "foreign" land. However, although we "might" suffer for Christ while in this non-Christian world, Peter reminds us that our inheritance and exaltation await us in our eternal homeland – our forever home.

Peter also wished that his readers capture this basic truth[6]: *by living an obedient, victorious life, even while under duress, a Christian can actually evangelize his hostile world.* Peter's message to believers of the First Century continues to speak to us today, reminding us of our heavenly hope and eternal inheritance in the midst of our sufferings. We are called to holiness and a consistent life of love that glorifies God and imitates Christ – no matter what. Even Martin Luther called this book one of the most outstanding books in the New Testament. He wrote, "He includes the true doctrine of faith – How Christ has been given to us, who takes away our sins and saves us."[7]

Peter writes that the end of all things is at hand (4:7) and reminds his readers that they are not to see themselves as criminals (4:15), but that they should take persecution as Christians (4:16), whose suffering is really part of the larger purpose of God. Peter advises that troubles were coming upon other brethren as well (5:9), but that a glorious end was in sight.

[8]The recipients of First Peter were most likely Gentiles, but we find that church leadership is also addressed in the last Chapter of the Epistle – I believe these church leaders were converted Gentiles. The reference to their former ignorance (1:14), and the futile ways inherited from their forefathers (1:18), suggests a pagan history that would not resonate with Jewish readers. Further, the former lifestyle of the readers (4:3-4) applies more to Gentiles rather than Jews.

Simon J. Kistermaker (1930-2017), a Dutch New Testament Scholar, wrote, "Considering the population...both Jews and Gentiles received the gospel of Christ and responded in faith to the call of the apostles. Jewish people...evangelized the Gentile population, so that many Gentiles were known to be God fearers...and became members in the church together with Jewish Christians."[9]

As we examine the Letter in totality, certain patterns begin to emerge, but it's only in the final chapters that we get to the meat and potatoes of what Peter is emphasizing. In 5:12, Peter wrote "*...I have written to you briefly, exhorting and testifying that this is the true grace of God. Stand firm in it!*" It is the expected (note *expected*) increase in the persecution of the Church that serves as the backdrop to the truth, and that it is via God's grace that Christ followers will be sustained as they experience the fiery ordeals to come. It's not "if" they will experience ordeals, but "when" they do.

The First Book of Peter may not be a doctrinal letter (although it is an awesome example of a Doctrine of Faith)[10], but the true value and treasure of the letter is found in the teaching and emphasis on maintaining faith in who we are as Christ followers, what He has promised, and who God is as our Creator, the one who elected us as His chosen. We are saved through the resurrected Christ, who will be given "*the sovereignty, the dominion, and the greatness of all the kingdoms under the whole heaven...and all the empires will serve and obey Him*" (Daniel 7:27). This is our inheritance as well, the twenty first century man.

3

Salutations and Greetings
1 Peter 1:1 - 12 (NASB)

PREMISE

[1]*God is the author of our salvation and has caused us to be born again to a Living Hope, Jesus Christ. Because of this, our faith in the Lord should be more precious to us than gold, with the outcome being nothing short of our trust in Him. Even the prophets of the Old Testament investigated the subject of the suffering and glory that the prophesied Christ would experience, yet they were told that they were not "serving themselves" but a future generation who would be blessed to hear the gospel preached to them.*

[2]*Peter was one of a unique group of men who was personally called and commissioned by Christ Himself, and who personally ministered with Christ both while He was walking the earth and after His*

resurrection. The Church was literally built upon the foundation of the teachings of these men.

First Peter Chapter 1

¹ I Peter, an apostle of Jesus Christ,

To those who reside as strangers, scattered throughout Pontus, Galatia, Cappadocia, Asia, and Bithynia, who are chosen ² according to the foreknowledge of God the Father, by the sanctifying work of the Spirit, to obey Jesus Christ and be sprinkled with His blood: May grace and peace be multiplied to you.

³ Blessed be the God and Father of our Lord Jesus Christ, who according to His great mercy has caused us to be born again to a living hope through the resurrection of Jesus Christ from the dead, ⁴ to *obtain* an inheritance *which is* imperishable, undefiled, and will not fade away, reserved in heaven for you, ⁵ who are protected by the power of God through faith for a salvation ready to be revealed in *the* last time. ⁶ In this you greatly rejoice, even though now for a little while, if necessary, you have been distressed by various trials, ⁷ so that the proof of your faith, being more precious than gold which perishes though tested by fire, may be found to result in praise, glory, and honor at the revelation of Jesus Christ; ⁸ and though you have not seen Him, you love Him, and though you do not see Him now, but believe in Him, you greatly rejoice with joy inexpressible and full of glory, ⁹ obtaining as the outcome of your faith, the salvation of your souls.

¹⁰ As to this salvation, the prophets who prophesied of the grace that *would come* to you made careful searches and inquiries, ¹¹ seeking to know what person or time the Spirit of Christ within them was indicating as He predicted the sufferings of Christ and the glories to follow. ¹² It was revealed to them that they were not serving themselves, but you, in these things which now have

been announced to you through those who preached the gospel to you by the Holy Spirit sent from heaven—things into which angels long to look.

Hello, Salutations and Greetings

In verse 1:1, Peter is speaking to both Jews and Gentiles who had converted to Christianity in the First Century, but I believe he was speaking more directly to converted Gentiles. Some commentary suggests that he was only talking to converted Jews[3] but if we review what Peter wrote in 1:14, it implies otherwise; "...*don't conform to evil desires that you had when you lived in ignorance.*" Ignorance in this case is a reference to those who had been living without the knowledge of God. Even though Jews had a problem with Jesus, they did believe in God. Gentiles, on the other hand, did not believe in one God, so while Peter was writing to Jews and Gentiles, I take it that Peter was focused more directly on converted Gentiles.

The believers (Christ followers) that Peter was writing to were located in four provinces of the Roman Empire, which are now part of modern-day Turkey – and they were apparently going through high levels of stress due to persecution. In the context of this scripture, Peter was referring to the believers as "strangers" (exiles), not as pilgrims, refugees, or the equivalent of modern-day expats; he was also speaking to them in recognition as God's "chosen" (elect), meaning His chosen people. Some translations, such as the NASB version referenced in this chapter, use the words "strangers" and "chosen", but other translations use the words "exiles" and "elect", as

31

indicated in the parentheses. Note: the modern NASB version was updated and now includes the word "aliens" in place of "strangers", which my hardcopy NASB version says. Either way, the original Greek word used in the text for "exiles" or "strangers" or "aliens" is *parepidemos*, which refers to someone who is not passing through but settling down next to the native people.

⁴Just like God referred to Israel in the Old Testament, Peter was referring to Christians who had been chosen by God for salvation. Peter was providing HOPE for those living in a world that was not their own, recognizing that Heaven is the true home of all believers. He was speaking to people who were living in two Kingdoms.

⁵The Greek word for "chosen" or "elect" is *eklektos,* which applies not only to the people Peter was writing to at that time, but also to those who would receive Christ in the future (see Matthew 24:31, Mark 13:22), during the future tribulation (see Matthew 24:22, Mark 13:20), as well as holy/unfallen angels (see 1 Timothy 5:21). When used within scripture, *eklektos* reminds us that our election by God was thoughtful and deliberate, intended to bring us comfort when we feel that we are under persecution.

⁶Peter explicitly teaches within his writings that the Church of Jesus Christ is the new Israel. "Scattered" or "Dispersed," as used in verse 1, is typically used to describe the scattering of the Jews throughout the world, but Peter sees a parallel in the church also being dispersed throughout the known world – not just today in the 21st Century, but even during the 1st Century.

Peter's reference to such people in their "spiritual position" as the elect, rather than being "of the world" sets the tone for the remainder of the Epistle. As one of Jesus' chosen Apostles, Peter was concerned for them and wanted to prepare them to set their expectations for what many believe is a reference to coming calamities (on par with the holocaust, as some commentators suggest).

The phrases used in verse 1:2 enlighten us as to what Peter means when he calls the believers "elect exiles." Peter describes his readers as God's elected people because of God's foreknowledge (meaning that He knew ahead of time), that He set His covenantal love upon them in advance[7], which is the fundamental basis of salvation. It is His divine foreknowledge that serves as the basis on which a believer is chosen.

According to Romans 9:11, a believer's election (being chosen) is not based on anything within the person, but according to God's purpose...because of Him who calls (invites). This might be a difficult concept to grasp at first, but being chosen according to God's foreknowledge does not mean that His election is based on His knowledge of who would someday believe and who wouldn't. God invites everyone, implying that God may even call or invite those that He has foreknowledge will deny His invitation. So, how would the purpose of God relate to His foreknowledge? While verse 1:2 says that believers are chosen according to foreknowledge, we can reconcile this with God's purpose in other scriptures, such as Romans 9:11.

Romans 9:11 (NASB): "for the twins were not yet born and had not done anything good or bad, so that God's purpose according to His choice would stand, not because of works but because of Him who calls…"

The implication is that, even though unborn children haven't yet done anything good or bad, God still fully intends to carry out His purpose of selection, which is not based on works or what you can do, or whether what you've done was bad or good, but simply based on who He invites. That's it. God doesn't decree all things, meaning He doesn't force or dictate, but He allows for humans to make their own choices. This means that you and I have made, or will make, a choice to answer His call, and that He will not make the choice for you; even though He already has foreknowledge of what your choice will be.

Have you ever invited someone to an event, or a party, already knowing (you foreknew) that they would not, or could not, attend? You likely invited this person because you loved and respected them enough to invite them anyway. Romans 11:2 is another verse that points to the idea that the mere knowledge of something known by God in advance doesn't stop Him from lovingly caring for His children anyway. Paul rightly points out that God did not reject Israel even though He foreknew the choices they would make.[8] This lends strength to the idea that "fore-known," when used in salvation passages like Romans 11:2 and 1 Peter 1:2, might be more accurately portrayed as "fore-loved."[9]

Romans 11:2 (NASB): "God has not rejected His people whom he foreknew. Or do you not know what the Scripture says in the passage about Elijah, how he pleads with God against Israel?"

Or "*God has not rejected His people whom He fore-loved...*"

One commentary[10] suggested that "foreknowledge" means that God has preplanned everything, including your salvation, not that He just knew your choices before you made them. If this were the case, then the implication is that Christians are foreknown for salvation in the exact same way that Christ was foreordained "before the foundation of the world to be a sacrifice for sins." I earnestly believe that there is a tactical misrepresentation in this buried in the truth. If you read "foreknowledge" in this manner, then you might be left believing that God preplanned for some of us to be saved and some of us to not be saved, even before we were born. Did God "know" what your choices would be ahead of time? I believe so, yes. Does this mean that He planned your choices, or programmed them in you before you were born? Absolutely not – this is not possible from a loving Father who values your freedom of choice.

I believe that choices made by lost people are often the result of what and how they were taught, educated, and trained by misaligned, misinformed, and ignorant people (those that deny or do not know God). Therefore, it may be more precise to say that we are programmed by people around us that we "allow" to influence us – you choose to believe them. Only the Holy Spirit can save us from this type of programming, which is why the Lord calls ALL of us and why He places people into our lives through whom the Holy Spirit can operate in order to change our mind, and then our heart. This includes placing people like you and me in the lives of others, to show them the truth. You might be the one to help reach someone who is lost.

Some theological and denominational factions believe and teach on the idea of Predestination (covered more in Chapter 5).[11] Predestination implies that the life and decisions of a person are predestined by God from the day they are conceived [or born]; that you are born for a destiny that is completely beyond your control. I wrote an article in 2019 for *Rejoice Essentials* magazine about the idea of Judas Iscariot and his betrayal of Jesus titled "The Pawn of Judas Iscariot." Predestination presumes that Judas was born to betray Jesus; it was his foreordained destiny and he had no choice. This implies that Judas was nothing but a tool for God; this would suggest that Judas was a helpless pawn, unable to resist the invasion of satan into his life. That certainly is not the case, as even Judas himself conceded. He never said: "I could not help myself; Satan made me do it!" Rather, he confessed: "*I have sinned in that I have betrayed innocent blood*" (Matthew 27:4). It was in God's plan from the beginning that Jesus would be betrayed; if it wasn't Judas, it would have been someone else.

God foreknew that Judas, exercising his own freewill, would betray His Son. In John 13:18 and 17:12, we read where Jesus said that the actions of Judas were so "*that the scripture might be fulfilled.*" It is most likely that He was quoting from Psalm 41:9, where David was referring to someone who had turned against him, "*Even my close friend in whom I trusted, who ate my bread, has lifted his heel against me.*" When Jesus cited this passage, He omitted "whom I trusted" because He *"knew from the beginning who they were that did not believe, and who it was who would betray him"* (John 6:64). The Lord knew the heart of Judas.

The frequent rationalization, "I can't help what I do; I was predestined to do it," is stinkin-thinkin, but one that is readily accepted in a modern world that seeks to escape from personal responsibility. The scriptures teach that men will give an account on the Day of Judgment for their own conduct (Romans 14:12; 2 Corinthians 5:10), not for actions thrust upon them by God. How would this accounting work for Judas if he was predestined (or born) to sin against Jesus? The very idea is an insult to God. All of this is to argue that God did not preplan or control you to accept Him anymore than He preplanned or controlled those who rejected Him. We did it all of our own freewill and personal choices.

Peter continues his letter in verse 1:2 by stating *"by the sanctifying work of the Spirit,"* which is the process by which being "chosen" is made a reality – to be set apart. Believers are sanctified, set apart from sin, so that they are able to obey Jesus Christ.[12] You cannot obey Christ when operating in sin, which is why we are sanctified and set apart "from sin." This is awesome!

Peter refers to sanctification, which is "to make holy." You can think of the sanctification of the Spirit as your conversion to Christianity and to the gradual progress you will make in your Christian life for the remainder of your life on earth (1 Thessalonians 4:1, 3). Sanctification is the process that begins at the exact moment you accept the call of God to be part of the elect. It's the time of your

Justification (1 Corinthians 6:11): your justification was a single act and not a process.[13]

> *1 Thessalonians 4:1, 3: "[1]Finally then, brethren, we request and exhort you in the Lord Jesus, that as you received from us instruction as to how you ought to walk and please God (just as you actually do walk), that you excel still more... [3]For this is the will of God, your **SANCTIFICATION**; that is, that you abstain from sexual immorality..." (emphasis mine)*

> *1 Corinthians 6:11: "Such were some of you; but you were washed, but you were sanctified, but you were **JUSTIFIED** in the name of the Lord Jesus Christ and in the Spirit of our God" (emphasis mine).*

When Peter tells his readers that their (and our) "choosing," and "election" is *"by the sanctifying work of the spirit, that you may obey Christ"* (1:2), he is saying that salvation involves a continuous work of God within the believer, and it is not merely a process of getting a person into heaven.[14] Let's be clear: you and I weren't saved just to get into Heaven – this is a selfish and immature mindset – no, you were saved so that God can operate in and through you. This implies that we are now duty bound to obey Christ and, just like we were saved, to help save others [using whatever gifts God has given us].

Christians were chosen by God to have a covenant relationship with Him that is a further characterization of our obedience. We can't separate sanctification from obedience (obedience automatically comes with sanctification)[15]; if you fail to acknowledge this, you will very likely have problems later. Obedience to Jesus Christ refers to both your conversion when you confessed Jesus as your Lord and Savior – you were obedient to Him when He called you – as well as a reference to God's purpose for your life, with the idea that you are obeying Christ every day as you live out your life. But, the truth is, not all Christians are fully obedient. We do, and will, fail Him occasionally. We are never perfect, but always being perfected.

Unfortunately, there are people who separate themselves from the world in some blind effort to somehow be holier; but they are ignoring the command (meaning that they are being disobedient) to make disciples of all the nations (Matthew 28:19). While it may be absolutely necessary to separate ourselves from certain worldly things and activities (including stuff we might enjoy), we cannot obey Christ AND separate ourselves from people.[16]

> *Matthew 28:19: "Go therefore and make disciples of all the nations, baptizing them in the name of the Father and the Son and the Holy Spirit..."*

"Sprinkled with His blood" from 1:2 is a reference to Moses' act of sprinkling sacrificial "lambs'" blood on the people of Israel, which served as a symbol of sealing their covenant as a promise to obey God's word. In the New Covenant, faith in the shedding of Christ's blood on the cross not only activates God's promise of perfect atonement for sin for the believer – you and me – but also brings the believer into the New Covenant with Christ as we promise to obey the Lord and His word.[17] Faith here implies that you truly believe as fact

that: Christ is who He says He is, what He did on the cross, and why He did it.

Sprinkling with His blood refers to Christ's atoning work on the cross where all of the believer's sins were washed away (ALL). Atoning is the action of making a correction of the past, no matter how bad it was, and that correction has been made good. Additionally, under the Old Covenant, because of the fall of man which started with Adam, men were living separated from God (meaning spirit to Spirit) while also living under The Law. Jesus' "atoning" work on the cross resolved that separation and brought [*all*] men back into covenant with God — hence, the title New Covenant (or New Testament). As men, the past of being disconnected from God has been corrected (we now live connected to God spirit to Spirit). Faith here implies that you truly believe as fact that you have a direct connection to God. It is critical to understand this basic principle as you move through the rest of Peter's letter.

It is Christ's blood that brings believers into a relationship with Him. Peter sees believers "sprinkled" with the blood of Christ, referring to their covenant with God established through the initial Justification, and to subsequent cleansings by the blood of Christ through the ongoing process of sanctification, including regular acts of forgiveness and repentance. According to 1 John 1:9, "*If we confess our sins, He is faithful and righteous to forgive us our sins and to cleanse us (via His blood) from all unrighteousness.*"

"Peter concludes his rather long salutation at the end of verse 2 by wishing his readers grace and peace. [18]" Grace is an act that God does for us that we can't do for ourselves (i.e., we cannot save ourselves, so God, by grace, saves us by faith). The peace He wishes for his readers is peace in the midst of their stress and suffering; this is a peace that we always have because we have been reconciled to God and thus, have peace with Him.

Praise God to be Born Again to a Living Hope

In the NASB and KJV translations, amongst others, Peter opens verse 1:3 by offering a blessing to God (there are some translations, such as the NIV, that open with "Praise to God"). This is Peter's way of honoring God and praising Him for "causing" us to be born again into a new hope through the resurrection of Jesus Christ[19]. God has given believers, you and me, a new life and a guarantee of a future glory.

The guarantee that results from our being born again is that we have now acquired a part of the eternal inheritance that is reserved for us in heaven. We will be delivered to heaven through our faith in the gospel because we chose to believe in Christ, what He did on the cross, why He did it, and what happened as a result of His resurrection. And this, my brothers and sisters, is the meat and potatoes of the First Epistle of Peter. A Living Hope in a world that is not our own, a Living Hope that is still working with the 21st Century man.

Peter continues verse 1:3 by reminding us of God's "great mercy," but we can't talk about God's mercy without also talking about His grace. "Mercy is what God doesn't do to us even though we deserve it (He doesn't condemn us), while grace is what God does for us even though we don't deserve it (He saves us)[20]." Therefore, mercy is the remedy for the sins we have committed, while grace is the protection we have for sins that we haven't yet committed (but surely will). This is further supported in Hebrews 4:16.

> *Hebrews 4:16: "Therefore let us draw near with confidence to the throne of grace, so that we may receive mercy and find grace to help in time of need."*
>
> Or *"that we may receive the remedy for our current situation and find the protection we need to help us in our upcoming time of need."*

Our salvation only happens because of God's mercy, His grace, and His sovereignty, as He gave us a new life when we were "born again," and at that moment were justified. Born again is theologically referred to as regeneration (the moment we are remade at the time of our justification), the act by which God restores spiritual life to all of us who were once spiritually dead in sin because we were living separate from God, without the spirit-to-Spirit connection.

This new birth is only possible because God views those who accept and believe in Christ as being united with Christ in His resurrection. Without Jesus' resurrection, there wouldn't be anything for us on which to base either our faith or our hope in an eternal life after our physical death. This hope we have...is living in the form of Jesus. This means that Christ followers should have a hope for the future that is unshakeable because the resurrection of Christ is a promise of our own future resurrection (see Romans 8:11).

Our hope in the Living Hope of Jesus Christ allows us to live our lives in confident optimism and expectation because it:[21]

1. Comes from God.
2. Is a gift of grace.
3. Is defined by scripture.
4. Is a reasonable reality.
5. Is secured by the resurrection of Jesus Christ.
6. Is confirmed in the Christian by the Holy Spirit.
7. Defends the Christian against satan's attacks.
8. Is confirmed through trials.
9. Produces joy.
10. Is fulfilled in Christ's return.

Verse 1:4 carries over from the discussion of hope in verse 3, which is now described as an "inheritance," where Peter reminds us that we are heirs of God and joint heirs with Christ (see Rom 8:17). This is the logical consequence of being a child of God through the new birth that Peter has been describing.[22]

> *Romans 8:17: "and if children, heirs also, heirs of God and fellow heirs with Christ, if indeed we suffer with Him so that we may also be glorified with Him."*

Peter was showing the elect exiles, who were being persecuted, how to look past their current troubles to their eternal inheritance in the future (this applies to us today as well). [23]"Our heavenly inheritance is life, righteousness, joy, peace, perfection, God's presence, Christ's glorious companionship, rewards, and everything else God has planned." This allows us to manage our expectations because of our faith and hope for the future.

Matthew 25:34: "Then the King will say to those on his right, 'Come, you who are blessed by my Father; take your inheritance, the kingdom prepared for you since the creation of the world.'"

Colossians 1:12: "and giving joyful thanks to the Father, who has qualified you to share in the inheritance of his holy people in the kingdom of light."

Hebrews 9:15: "For this reason Christ is the mediator of a new covenant, that those who are called may receive the promised eternal inheritance—now that he has died as a ransom to set them free from the sins committed under the first covenant."

According to Ephesians 1:14, it's the indwelling Holy Spirit, the first installment, that is the guarantee of that inheritance. The mention of a first installment implies that there are additional installments.

*Ephesians 1:14: "who [**the Holy Spirit**] is a first installment of our inheritance, in regard to the redemption of God's own possession, to the praise of His glory" **(added for clarity)**.*

Anything and everything we gain or inherit on this earth will always, at some point, fade away. By contrast, our eternal inheritance is undefiled, meaning it's unpolluted and unstained with evil. It can't decay, it can't be tarnished, and it can't be extinguished.

Verse 1:4 ends with "you" and verse 1:5 continues with the thought, "[YOU], *who are protected by the power of God through faith for a salvation ready to be revealed in the last time.*" Not only is the inheritance from verse 4 secure, but so are all of us as believers secure[24]. The power of God, a power that stands ready to fight the evil intentions of the devil, is the exact same power that maintains our faith. "Salvation" in verse 5 continues the description of the "inheritance" from verse 4 and the "hope" of verse 3 – but here salvation is stated in a future tense.

This salvation will "be revealed" in a future time, a reference to an end time; it's an accomplished fact – it's already been prepared and it's ready. So, we have now seen salvation used in three tenses in only five verses: 1) The Past, with the act of your Justification, 2) The Present, with your ongoing process of Sanctification, and 3) The Future, which will be your Glorification. Peter is making reference to salvation in verse 5 as pertaining to your future glorification, and the exact moment you will actually receive your inheritance. We are saved now/today, but we are simply waiting for the final eradication of sin in our future resurrected body. "The "last time" at the end of verse 5 refers to the coming of Christ, a time of the gathering of both living and dead believers in the air[25]"(1 Thessalonians 4:13-18).

> *1 Thessalonians 4:13-18: "[13] But we do not want you to be uninformed, brethren, about those who are asleep, so that you will not grieve as do the rest who have no hope. [14] For if we believe that Jesus died and rose again, even so God will bring with Him [Jesus] those who have fallen asleep [died] in Jesus. [15] For this we say to you by the word of the Lord, that we who are alive and remain until the coming of the Lord, will not precede those who have fallen asleep. [16] For the Lord Himself will descent from heaven with a shout, with the voice of the archangel and with the trumpet of God, and the dead in Christ will rise first. [17] Then we who are alive and remain will be caught up together with them in the clouds to meet the Lord in the air, and so we shall*

always be with the Lord. [18] *Therefore comfort one another with these words."*

Note: the study of end-times prophecy is known as Eschatology, where the debate of a rapture and end time events continues. That is NOT the purpose of this commentary of First Peter, but Peter is nonetheless talking about end time events (whatever your personal eschatology, or end-time belief, happens to be).

Peter is trying to shift the focus of our minds to what is going to be revealed in the end times. He is reminding us that God will protect us by sustaining our faith all of the way to the end (Peter is referring specifically to our faith, not our physical bodies). Only we can give up our faith; that is our choice. But God will never give up.

It is God's supreme power, His omniscience and His omnipotence, that is sovereign over our future inheritance, but He is also keeping the believer secure in their faith, today. No one can steal your inheritance, and no one can disqualify you from receiving it (only you can disqualify yourself)[26]. The believer's response, yours and mine, to God's election and the Spirit's conviction is faith, but even our faith is given to us by God (see Ephesians 2:8). And it is our continued faith in God that is the evidence of God's abiding power. At the moment of our salvation through the justification, God energized our faith and He continues to preserve it. It is permanent and it never dies [only we can give it up].

> *Ephesians 2:8 (NASB): "For by grace you have been saved through faith; and this is not of yourselves, it is the gift of God…"*

In 1:6, "Peter says that believers should *"greatly rejoice"* at the prospect"[27] of being part of the elect, God's mercy and grace, our salvation, and our inheritance. Our rejoicing is expected to more than compensate for those moments when we are being *"distressed by various trials;"* peirasmois in the Greek, also meaning "temptations." These trials are only temporary, though it may not feel like it at the time.

To be exceedingly glad or exuberantly jubilant is a kind of joy that is not based on constantly changing or temporal circumstances; but it is a kind of joy that comes from an unchanging, eternal relationship with God. Peter relates this joy to 1) the assurance that our eternal inheritance is protected, and 2) the assurance from one's proven faith.

Peter teaches several important principles about trials, or trouble, in this verse:[28]

1. Trouble does not last.
2. Trouble serves a purpose.
3. Trouble brings turmoil.
4. Trouble comes in various forms.
5. Trouble should not diminish the Christian's joy.

Rejoicing in trials (see James 1:2-4), serves as "the proof of [their] faith" as Peter's thought continues into verse 7.[29]

> *James 1:2-4: "2 Consider it all joy, my brethren, when you encounter various trials, 3 knowing that the testing of your faith produces endurance. 4 And let endurance have its perfect result, so that you may be perfect and complete, lacking in nothing."*

Peter goes on to show, in verse 1:7, how it is the hope of salvation that ought to give a believer endurance during trials [*and temptations*], a message that he continues through to verse 1:9. God doesn't need proof of faith from us, but people regularly feel that it is necessary to prove their faith to God [and themselves][30], so Peter's reference to "proof of faith" is more for our benefit as a form of evidence and encouragement as we experience trials and tribulations.

When we face a trial or feel personally persecuted, we may experience a degree of fear or uncertainty causing us to stumble for a moment, but this is okay; our faith eventually overcomes this temporary uncertainty. As we continue to face trials in the future, it's our recollection of past victories over fear and doubt that give us greater confidence and consistency in exercising our faith in the present.

Peter compares a believer's faith to gold, in fact, much more valuable than gold. But even the real value of gold isn't realized until it's been smelted, refined, and tested by fire, making it pure and, as a result, precious. There are no easy shortcuts to remove the dross and impurities in the metal that deplete its value: fire is necessary. If we replace the word "gold" with "faith," we get the following:

> *"Faith's real value won't be realized until it has been tried and refined. Faith that has been "tested by fire" is pure and precious and there are no shortcuts or easy ways to remove the dross and impurities." ~ William Baker (The Books of James & Peter)*

The metaphor of comparing faith with gold being "tested by fire" is something that has been written and taught on, extensively for centuries; it's a phrase that is even used frequently in secular environments. It is a reference to the refining of metals and is a very appropriate description for the testing of a believer's faith.

When smelting metals, the smelter removes the impurities that float to the surface and discards them, allowing the metal to become purer. When it comes to the idea of faith, the impurities include your "fears, uncertainties, and your doubts" (Baker, 2004) that come to the surface during times that test your faith. As the process of removing these impurities from your life continues over time, your faith becomes brighter, purer, and stronger. What's left is a deposit, one that will *result in praise and glory and honor at the revelation of Jesus Christ,*

The lesson in your personal "smelting" process is:

1. Gold tested by fire is more valuable.
2. Faith is "spiritual" gold.
3. Faith tested by fire enhances its nature, just like gold.
4. Only faith tested by fire is genuine faith. Anyone can say they have faith until the time comes that they need it.
5. The process of being tested by fire brings forth the gift of grace – assistance and strength gifted from God that allows us to grow.
6. When we are tested by fire, this is when Jesus is revealed in our lives.
7. We "rejoice" when tested by fire. When our faith is tested, the impurities of our old self are removed and thrown away, allowing our faith to become purer (which serves as evidence and encouragement when we experience future trials).

This kind of faith is the physical manifestation of God's power in us, which serves as evidence of the revelation of who Jesus Christ is. Accordingly and rightfully so, this deserves an honest and obvious question: does God allow troubles to occur? If so, what would His purpose be? God's purpose in allowing trouble may be to test the reality of one's faith; and if this is the case, the benefit of such a testing by fire would be for the Christian's benefit, not for God as alluded to earlier. When you and I come through a trial still trusting in our Lord Jesus Christ, we are assured that our faith is genuine (it's made purer). If there is one thing a 21st Century man needs more than ever, it's the "pure" confidence in his faith. Faith is where the 21st Century man finds HOPE while living in two kingdoms.

The degree of confidence you have in your faith gives you a hope that non-believers believe isn't rational; to them it is fake and not logical. It's odd, but also not surprising, how confidence due to faith in the Lord actually makes some unbelievers angry. In verse 1:8, Peter is reminding us that, even though we can't physically see Jesus Christ, we still LOVE Him anyway; we still believe in Him and we are filled with joy about Him in the process. This belief in Him produces HOPE, meaning that our FAITH (our belief) is a result while hope is a product. Therefore, LOVE is the catalyst that sets the foundation of FAITH, in which our HOPE is constructed and built upon.

> *1 Corinthians 13:4-7: "Love is patient, love is kind... It does not act discracefully, it does not seek its own benefit...it keeps every confidence, it believes [faith] all things, hopes all things, endures all things." (added for clarity)*

> *Hebrews 11:1: "Now faith is the assurance of things hoped for, the conviction of things not seen."*

Love, Faith, and Hope operate together. Too many in Christian environments try to categorize them into their own unique boxes (I sure did). Without love, your faith and your hope would not be pure, at best, your faith and hope are at risk of being misguided. Nonetheless, without all three operating in your life, your Christian walk will be chaotic and problematic, and make you susceptible to false and misleading teachings – creating a spiritual environment of misdirection. A true relationship with Jesus Christ requires that LOVE, FAITH, and HOPE all be operating together: in, and through, your life.

If we have no hope, then we need to check our faith by examining where our faith is placed and rooted. Is your faith placed on Jesus Christ and rooted in love? Our faith is established [it's locked in] based on our perceptions, and the reality, of our past and our present; whereas hope is looking to the reality of the future - we are expectant. Christ followers are people of love, faith and hope, they are not fear minded, doubtful, nor uncertain of the future. This is also why young Christians will rely on the faith of others for a period of time - but not too long - as they adjust to their new life. During the early years of a Christians walk, the foundation of faith is being built and hardened (think of concrete), where the 21st Century Man will increase his own faith and establish his hope, all rooted in love as he builds his own independent relationship with Jesus.

Peter is also trying to tell us in 1:8 that love can exist even when we can't see it while smack dab in the middle of trials or tribulation, or when we are being tempted. Think about a person who you may be struggling with in your life, someone that just seems to consistently make you angry or irritable – can you see any qualities in that person that allow you to love that person? God does. This is sometimes referred to as gratitude, and is a sure sign of love.

Non-believers will often confess, or even vow, that they will finally believe in Jesus if He would manifest right in front of them. I know I did and I also know that I wasn't being honest when I said it. I was being sarcastic and cynical. I most likely wouldn't have believed He was Jesus even if He did pop up right in front of me; I probably would have thought He was an alien as I held a stronger belief in aliens than I did in Jesus. The truth is that we aren't going to love Jesus more just because we can physically see Him (the Pharisees are proof of this); though I am confident that we wouldn't be disappointed. But what can be seen is the manifestation and the result of who Jesus is, and this can only be accomplished through people like you and me.

Peter describes this present relationship with Christ as one that causes the believer to *"greatly rejoice with joy inexpressible and full of glory.*[31]*"* We often confuse the idea of joy with the idea of happiness. Our joy is not dependent on our circumstances, nor is our joy dependent on being happy; but it is true, in some cases, that our happiness may be impacted based on our circumstances as well as the amount of joy we have.

Joy is not something that is reserved for the future; joy can protect a believer's faith through all kinds of trials in the present – even if you meander off the path for a few minutes. The believer is filled with joy, and glory, simply because of this hopeful expectation that we see in Jesus – no matter what our present circumstances may be.

"The outcome of your faith" from 1:9 is another reference to the future, our glorification, or the culmination of the sanctification process, that we have spent our entire Christian lives experiencing, the finalization of the aspect of the believer's salvation. The word used here, *"outcome,"* is the Greek word *telos*, which means "completion." Peter is referring to the goal of your faith and why you have faith in the first place. A true believer who is facing trials knows the ultimate outcome – that "his or her salvation is never in jeopardy" (Baker, pg. 107). When we depart the earth, we will head home and the outcome will be that we are complete.

However, the word *"obtaining"* in verse 9 is a current, present, and ongoing action. In one sense, Christians now possess the result of their faith, a constant deliverance from the power of sin. In another sense, we are waiting to receive the full salvation of eternal glory in the redemption of our bodies (see Romans 8:23)[32].

> *Romans 8:23: "And not only this, but also we ourselves, having the first fruits of the Spirit, even we ourselves groan within ourselves, waiting eagerly for our adoption as sons, the redemption of our body."*

Verse 9 completes the end of a thought as Peter will soon begin to talk about a different perspective on the idea of our salvation, although many translations make no note of this transition. After finishing one idea in verse 9, Peter moves on to another idea in verse 10. Baker (2004) refers to verses 1:10-12 as a kind of an "oh by the way" idea, that connects the idea of salvation discussed in the previous verses to the ideas of salvation as prophesied in the Old Testament.

Peter indicates that the idea of a future salvation was somewhat of a mystery to the Old Testament prophets who themselves prophesied about it (Isaiah and Zechariah, for example). They could only speculate on what God was revealing to them as they reviewed and pondered over certain statements given to them by the Holy Spirit because they were told of a "grace that would come," a reference to the coming of Jesus Christ that was summed up with the idea of "grace." They only knew that it would be by God's grace that the Messiah would be sent into the world, but they had no idea when or how.

The idea that the Old Testament prophets "searched" and "inquired," as pointed out by Peter in 1:10, simply implies their lack of knowledge as to how the prophecies would be fulfilled, not that they wouldn't or what the prophecies themselves meant.[33]

God is by nature gracious, and He was the same God during the times of the Old Covenants (such as the Abrahamic and Mosaic Covenants), which all came with conditions. But the prophets foretold an even greater display of grace than they themselves had ever known or would experience. The prophets spent time studying their own writings of the time in an attempt to learn more about the promised salvation. Though they believed they were personally saved from their sin by their faith, there was no way they could fully fathom what would be involved in the life-and-death accomplishment of Jesus Christ.

The Old Testament prophets were seeking to know the person that the Holy Spirit was telling them about: "Who would this person be?" and "When would He come?" Even though they couldn't see when their prophecies would happen, they did know that Christ would suffer, and they knew that He would be glorified.

In 1:12, Peter concludes his "oh, by the way…" thought by sharing that, even though the prophets didn't receive the specific answers they wanted, it was revealed to them that they were not serving themselves but people in the future – people like you and me[34]. The prophets understood that their prophecies concerned the future and what they were proclaiming would not occur during their immediate lifetimes.

Can you imagine how this made them feel? I have no doubt that they were telling themselves, "I want it now, not tomorrow," yet they still maintained their faith in a future hope. Kind of like us today, who know of the second coming of Christ; we want Him to come now, yet we still maintain our faith in confident expectation of His future arrival (whether or not in our own lifetime). The prophets knew that they were serving a future age that would experience what is known as the "First Advent" (the birth of Christ) as well as a time in the distant future that would we know as the "Second Advent" (Christ's Second Coming).

In these first twelve opening verses if his letter, Peter is stating that God's salvation of humankind is a very targeted lesson concerning the grace of God, a grace that is neither available to the angels who disobeyed and fell from heaven, nor to those that deny Him or mock the Gospel. Peter is sharing what believers of that time had already been hearing but needed a reminder – the good news of the Gospel that had been proclaimed to them and had changed them in the first place. We today, men of the 21st Century, need this reminder as well because the struggle is real.

The Old Testament people of God did not know Christ or the Gospel, but they did believe in the promises that God had revealed to them which pointed to a future Christ. The New Testament apostles and preachers of the gospel had the privilege of proclaiming that the prophecies written by the Old Testament prophets had come to pass (see 2 Corinthians 6:1-2). Even as the New Testament apostles and preachers of the New Testament "had" the privilege of proclaiming, we today still "have" the privilege of proclaiming.

> *2 Corinthians 6:1-2:* "And working together *with Him*, we also urge you not to receive the grace of God in vain— 2 for He says,
>
> 'AT A FAVORABLE TIME I LISTENED TO YOU,
> AND ON A DAY OF SALVATION I HELPED YOU.'
> Behold, now is 'A FAVORABLE TIME,' behold, now is
> 'A DAY OF SALVATION.'"

4

A Call to be Holy
1 Peter 1:13 - 2:3 (NLT)

<u>PREMISE</u>

Peter's letter proclaims that followers of Christ should rejoice in suffering because it is their suffering that validates their faith, ensuring that their faith is pure and honest. Christ followers already know the fulfillment of the Old Testament prophesies, all of which point to Christ. Do you, or can you, remain faithful to your salvation through Jesus, no matter what your earthly circumstances may happen to be? Or is there a breaking point where your faith will fail and you backslide into a sinful life, the person you were before Christ?

When God caused us to be born again, He was giving us a new birth as part of His provision in salvation. The reason God provided us with salvation is simply because He is merciful; we all need His mercy because we were in a pitiful, desperate, wretched condition as sinners when He called us. In this letter, Peter is personalizing the Christian's intimate relationship with God through Jesus. It is as heirs with Christ and children of God that we must always prepare our minds for action while keeping our spirits sober against the worldly behaviors and beliefs we were ignorant about during the period of our lives "before Christ."

Peter is reminding us that due to this personal relationship with Jesus, we are considered saints and should behave as such in fear of God as opposed to fear of man, knowing that He will, someday, judge us all for what we've done (including those that denied Him)[1]. While we physically walk the earth, Peter is telling us that we are to live, distinctly, as a people who belong to God, in a condition of holiness. It is our future inheritance waiting for us in heaven that should serve as one of the major incentives for us to operate in holiness as God intended – no matter what.

We also keep our hope on the inheritance of grace that will be ours when we are finally glorified at the second coming of Christ[2]. It is this inheritance that has been promised that should motivate believers to set their hope entirely on their future and to live in fear of God, who redeemed us at the cost of His own son.

Since we have been given a new life by the word of God, we are to love one another fervently. We should long for God's word in such a way that we will continue to grow in our faith for the remainder of our Christian lives on earth.

First Peter Chapter 1 (cont'd)

[13] So prepare your minds for action and exercise self-control. Put all your hope in the gracious salvation that will come to you when Jesus Christ is revealed to the world. [14] So you must live as God's obedient children. Don't slip back into your old ways of living to satisfy your own desires. You didn't know any better then. [15] But now you must be holy in everything you do, just as God who chose you is holy. [16] For the Scriptures say, "You must be holy because I am holy."

[17] And remember that the heavenly Father to whom you pray has no favorites. He will judge or reward you according to what you do. So you must live in reverent fear of him during your time here as "temporary residents." [18] For you know that God paid a ransom to save you from the empty life you inherited from your ancestors. And it was not paid with mere gold or silver, which lose their value. [19] It was the precious blood of Christ, the sinless, spotless Lamb of God. [20] God chose him as your ransom long before the world began, but now in these last days he has been revealed for your sake.

[21] Through Christ you have come to trust in God. And you have placed your faith and hope in God because he raised Christ from the dead and gave him great glory.

[22] You were cleansed from your sins when you obeyed the truth, so now you must show sincere love to each other as brothers and sisters. Love each other deeply with all your heart.

[23] For you have been born again, but not to a life that will quickly end. Your new life will last forever because it comes from the eternal, living word of God. [24] As the Scriptures say,

"People are like grass;
    their beauty is like a flower in the field.
The grass withers and the flower fades.
[25] But the word of the Lord remains forever."

And that word is the Good News that was preached to you.

First Peter Chapter 2

So get rid of all evil behavior. Be done with all deceit, hypocrisy, jealousy, and all unkind speech. **2** Like newborn babies, you must crave pure spiritual milk so that you will grow into a full experience of salvation. Cry out for this nourishment, **3** now that you have had a taste of the Lord's kindness.

A Call to be Holy

One of the cool things about scripture is the constant "call to action" given within – if you look and discern carefully[3]. In 1:13, Peter gives us a clear call to prepare for action. In the original Greek, we are advised to "gird up the loins of the mind." "To gird up" means to prepare, which is how it is translated in the New Living Translation as seen in this chapter of my book. The expression "to have the loins girded" means to always be ready for anything, and is language typically used in regard to military preparation[4].

When preparing for battle, the first step Roman soldiers were required to take before battle was to "gird up" and tighten their belts in order to restrict the flow of their outer garments which might trip them up or get tangled in their weapons[5]. They needed to do this in order to be ready to move in a hurry, but in the case of this verse, Peter is actually making an analogy with our thought process.

Peter is not advising his readers to literally do what Roman soldiers did before battle; it is a metaphor for preparing our minds for the spiritual battles that will come in the middle of high stress and persecution. A more scriptural practice of girding our loins, or preparing our minds, is to keep our minds dominated by the word of God[6]. This gives us the readiness we need to fight the battle of the mind, which is where spiritual warfare really occurs.

A simple, yet personal, life example of this for me is in regard to traffic conditions on the roads. I hate traffic; I despise it. And if I am about to go somewhere knowing that the traffic will be horrible, my body tenses up and I stress even before getting on the road. If I don't prepare myself ahead of time before getting on the road, then I become "that guy" who gets angry and glares at the people around me (with perhaps even a few hand gestures – definitely unChristlike). However, if I spend a few minutes preparing myself for the inevitable traffic, meditating and calming myself down, I hit the road prepared for the battle ahead. When prepared, I am more relaxed, less irritable, and more forgiving of other drivers – and definitely no hand gestures! A simple example, but one that I am sure many can relate to.

Rick Renner, in *Sparkling Gems*, also observed that Peter is not talking about clothing but is referring to the "loins" of our minds, telling us that if we don't do the following, then we will allow things in and around our lives to hinder us and slow us down as we walk and run our race with God:[7]

- Deal with the loose ends that exist in our minds and emotions,
- Correct those parts of our thinking that we know are wrong,

- Grab hold of all those dangling areas in our thinking and put them out of the way,
- And remove them by the authority of the word of God.

In Ephesians 6:14, Paul calls upon believers to gird up their waists [loins] with truth with truth, meaning "reality pertaining to a matter." Paul is telling us to prepare ourselves with the truth and the reality of Jesus Christ. In 1:13, Peter is telling us to prepare our minds for anything, both emotionally and strategically. We are to reject the present challenges of the world while focused on God's intended future for us.

> *Ephesians 6:14 (NKJV): "Stand therefore, having girded your waist with truth, having put on the breastplate of righteousness..."*

To be successful in our spiritual lives (within our hearts), we must deal with the matter between our ears. When we don't spend time with God and meditate on His Word, then we are deliberately allowing the wrong type of thinking to occupy our minds; this can leak into our hearts, which then impacts our spirit.

In addition to preparing our minds, we need to "exercise self-control" – other translations state "keep sober *in spirit.*" "Sober" means to be watchful and circumspect, but "in spirit" is not in the original text (you won't see it in the KJV, for example)[8]; scholars point out that it was added later by translators to assist with understanding that Peter was referring to our mental faculties and not to alcohol. This includes the ideas of steadfastness, self-control, clarity of mind and moral decisiveness[9]. The sober Christian is someone in control of themselves, in charge of his priorities, and not emotionally excited by the various temptations of the world. This will be discussed multiple times throughout Peter's letter.

By keeping sober in spirit and maintaining self-control, we are fixing our hope completely on the grace and revelation of Jesus Christ; we are completely focused on the eventual victory of Jesus Himself and the completion of our salvation at His second coming[10]. We recognize that the times ahead will be daunting, but the reminder of His ultimate victory gives added courage during our trials. As a reminder, the premise of this letter from Peter is how to deal with suffering during times of high stress and persecution; hence the constant reminders about remaining focused on the things of God.

The Holy Spirit will work in you to get your attention when necessary, but we sometimes fail to realize that God is only trying to help us work out the problems of our lives ourselves, cooperating with the Holy Spirit that is already in us. The Lord has already equipped us and we sometimes fail to remember or realize this; if you pay attention and listen, you will take hold and allow Him to guide you. When this happens, you will focus on the right things and be able to move forward, and nothing can hold you back except you.

In 1:14, Peter is telling us that, as followers of God and His ways, we are to leave our old methods and ways of operating behind and we are to adopt God's standards of morality[11]. In our previous life "before Christ," we were ignorant of the ways of God, but now we are aware, so there is no excuse. Interestingly, in Romans, Paul has a particular perspective on the idea of being "ignorant" about God.

In Romans 1:18-32, Paul is telling us that the human conscience, which is part of our spirit, tells us the difference between right and wrong, but as we disregard and ignore what our conscience is telling us more and more, we will eventually suppress it altogether. Thus, according to Paul, the idea of being ignorant is not excusable and humanity doesn't have an excuse (Romans 1:20).[12]

> *Romans 1:20 (MSG): "By taking a long and thoughtful look at what God has created, people have always been able to see what their eyes as such can't see: eternal power, for instance, and the mystery of his divine being. So nobody has a good excuse."*

By writing about the readers that "didn't know any better then," in verse 14 (other translations write about those with a "previous ignorance of God"), Peter's reference suggests that the recipients of this letter were mostly Gentiles who, before coming to Christ, didn't know any better because they did not know about God. As Jews knew about God, they were not ignorant of God, so it is less likely that his message was for converted Jews. Paul's take in Romans 1:20 is an interesting contrast to Peter's in 1:14.

As believers, we are to fight against the temptations and desires to sin (there's that reference to battle again). Christ requires that believers live their lives in holiness by using what Rick Renner refers to as "spiritual common sense" [13] that keeps us from walking off of a dangerous cliff "spiritually." We are to be obedient and behave just like the Holy One who called us, for to be like Jesus means to be holy ourselves. It is our holiness that sets us apart from sin and contrasts our life "after Christ" with our previous life "before Christ." Can you see the difference?

If we are living in obedience and in a state of holiness, we are displaying the character of God, who can then use us to attract others in whom He is working to draw towards Him. This also means that we treat both God and His Word with deep respect and admiration. Too many men of the 21st Century are struggling with the preeminence of treating God and His Word with deep respect and admiration; while difficult, it is not impossible.

However, Peter is also pulling from Leviticus 11:44 and 19:2, making the act of being holy a relative one as it is impossible for humans to be perfectly holy, a mistake that some Christians make causing unnecessary frustration. Hopefully, this gives you some peace. Only God Himself is absolutely holy, but He still means business when He states His desire for us to have a substantial measure of holiness[14]. In the last analysis He knows your heart and He knows when you are giving it your best. If you are faking it or not giving it your full effort, He knows that too.

> Leviticus 11:44: "For I am the LORD your God. Consecrate yourselves therefore, and be holy, for I am holy. And you shall not make yourselves unclean with any of the swarming things that swarm on the earth."

> Leviticus 19:2: "Speak to all the congregation of the sons of Israel and say to them, 'You shall be holy, for I the LORD your God am holy.'"

Verse 1:17 reminds us that God does not play favorites; He is not grading us on a scale, but you should deliberately want to live a life of worshipping Him while you are alive on the earth. This verse is another way of saying, "If you are a Christian, then you are a believer who knows God, and God will judge your work fairly." As a believer, you will honor Him as your heavenly Father; you will respect Him and His evaluation of your life. If we truly want a relationship with Him, then it will come at the price of guarding our holiness.

In v.17, Peter is making reference to the final judgment, when all believers will be judged according to their deeds[15]. We fear God, but it is not a paralyzing type of fear; it is a fear of His discipline and His displeasure. In my 20 years of military service, I respected and held some military leaders in such high regard that I was literally afraid of letting them down and displeasing them. It is this type of reverence for God that should characterize our lives during our time on this earth.

Thomas R Schreiner notes, "God's tenderness and love as Father is mingled with His judgment and the fear that should mark Christians in this world. Thus, believers should live with a healthy reverence in all their conduct in the world."[16]

In verse 1:18, the NLT says, *"God paid a ransom"* to save us; other translations state that we have been *"Redeemed."* Either way, Peter is referring to the act of the believer receiving the ransom paid that set them free from their previous life of living in bondage to sin and the curse of the law.[17]

The NLT further states that our ransom was not paid with mere gold or silver *"which lose their value."* Other translations use words like "perishable" or "corruptible" to describe things that are physical and cannot bring salvation. While silver and gold can provide the perception of freedom while we walk the earth, this type of freedom is temporary; money is corruptible and can't bring freedom in the form of eternal salvation to anyone.

One of our motivations to live a life of holiness is the priceless redemption that we enjoy as believers. As such, we belong to Jesus because, as Peter points out in 1:19, He purchased us with His blood. Our previous life was destructive and leading us to a permanent death: it had no future[18], whereas a redeemed life is one where we live a life of joyful service and obedience to Christ along with the knowledge of the inheritance we will receive in eternity.

And here it is, the prime motivation for holiness in the face of believers: we were bought at the price of the precious blood of Jesus Christ. In the movie *Saving Private Ryan*, Tom Hanks plays a character who was mortally wounded in the act of saving Private Ryan, played by Matt Damon. As Matt Damon comforts Hanks as he slowly passes away, Tom tells him to "earn it." 50 years later, Private Ryan is now an old man standing near the grave of Tom Hanks' character as he states, "I did my best." If we are saved by another man who is killed in the process, would we not make every effort to make that man's sacrifice worth it? How much more should we make every effort for the One who sacrificed Himself for our eternity?

In most respects, we shouldn't need anything more than this, but the idea of an inheritance that awaits us in heaven doesn't hurt. Nonetheless, the fact that we have been delivered from a life of futility and meaninglessness is of super significance. It was Christ that broke the power of generational sins, those that are passed from father to son over generations. Yet, some still tend to treat their salvation as a cheap trifle when they forget what it cost Jesus. The reference to *"the sinless, spotless Lamb of God"* points to Jesus being unblemished and spotless. This shows us, emphatically, how much God values us that we are worth the price paid for our salvation. This is why Paul admonishes us in 1 Corinthians 6:19-20 when he reminds us that *"our bodies are a temple for the Holy Spirit, who is in us because of God, and that we are not our own. We were bought at a price and we need to glorify God with what He purchased"* – our body (i.e., our life).

As stated in the opening of this section – what other motivation for holiness do we need? To glorify God is to honor Him; therefore, why shouldn't we obey Him and strive for holiness?

In verse 1:20, Peter continues with his message about salvation through Jesus. He does so by tracing Jesus all of the way back to when the world was first created, stating that Jesus was known even before the foundation of the world. But, as Peter contends, Jesus appeared "physically" at the prescribed time for your sake, and mine. I agree with William Baker (2004) who believes that Jesus existed as the second headship of the trinity prior to His birth[19], but He was not the Son of God until His birth. It was this action of His birth that kicked off the transition to the New Covenant.

Most theologians and scholars agree that, in order for Christ to be the second person of the Trinity, it's not possible that the first time the Lord knew of Him was when He was conceived and born into existence as a human being[20]. Rather, Jesus already existed before He was born into this world and the Lord already knew Him. So for Christ to be "foreknown" must refer to an eternal covenant that was arranged beforehand, to provide for the salvation of those chosen [the elect].

Some evidence that suggests Jesus was present in the Old Testament can be found in Old Testament references to the priest Melchizedek as most believe this priest was, in fact, Jesus.

> *Genesis 14:19-20: "Melchizedek blessed Abram with this blessing: 'Blessed be Abram by God Most High, Creator of heaven and earth. And blessed be God Most High, who has defeated your enemies for you.' Then Abram gave Melchizedek a tenth of all the goods he had recovered."*

> *Psalm 110:4: "The Lord has sworn and will not change his mind, 'You are a priest forever after the order of Melchizedek.'"*

> *Hebrews 7:3: "He is without father or mother or genealogy, having neither beginning of days nor end of life, but resembling the Son of God he continues a priest forever."*

What does the Holy Spirit lead you to believe about the existence of Jesus before the New Covenant?

For Christians, it is because of Jesus and His works that we have our belief in God. This might seem odd when we consider that even non-Christians believe in God as Peter implies in 1:21. However, there is a difference between believing that God exists and believing in God[21]. Simply believing that God exists does not recognize the salvation that He provided for us, nor does this imply love of Him or require obedience. Even the devil knows that God exists, but he doesn't believe in Him and he is definitely not obedient.

We, too, as Christ followers believe that the devil exists, but we don't believe in the devil. Our faith and confidence are on God as we place our hope on the action of God raising Christ from the dead as a reminder of our own future reward. Believing in God is the belief that He provided us with our salvation in Christ[22]. Peter is furthering his discussion with verse 1:21: that God had planned, before creation, that He would send Christ and reveal Him at a particular point in time when believers lived so that they would be able to enjoy the privilege of living during a time of fulfillment.

Because we were cleansed from our sins, we are to love the brotherhood, no matter what[23]. God saved us by His mercy when we didn't deserve it; it is therefore unseemly and sinful for a believing brother not to love another brother. Brothers are to love one other fervently, which also means diligently and carefully – with all our heart. Therefore, we must guard our hearts from anything contrary to this type of love. And yet, men today break this covenant, primarily due to pride or through the trap of making comparison. Sadly, even Christian brothers are guilty.

This love of our brothers that Peter writes about in 1:22, has been firmly grounded at the time of our conversion, the day we were justified as part of our salvation. It is fraudulent not to love because someone whose soul has been purified by the blood of Jesus Christ only has the capacity to love this kind of love that requires meeting our brothers at the point of their need. Can you think of a few men, Christian men, who you despise? If you answered yes, then you are not living the way God ordains as we shouldn't even have the capacity to despise another brother.

Loving like God ordains us to love is operating in holiness as previously discussed in verses 1:15-17. It also implies that we live with valid concerns about our relationships with other brothers. Some men don't know what to do about concerns they have with relationships with some of their brothers. The answer is found throughout the New Testament: love is an act; love is not just a feeling. So, act on it. You can do it! This act of love for other brothers is part of the process of surviving, and living in faith, in a way that honors Christ during the times we are under high stress and persecution. The act of love includes loving those that are persecuting you.

The kind of love discussed in verse 1:22 is only possible because we have been born again by the seed of God that is imperishable – the living Word of God [24]– as Peter properly points out in verse 1:23. This rebirth and new spiritual life never fails and allows love to flow from us as members of God's family. At the exact moment we received Jesus Christ as our Lord and Savior, in faith, God put His Spirit and His Word in our hearts like a seed. But like all seeds, they require care and water to grow and flourish, in this case, via a relationship with Jesus Himself.

I believe there is a direct correlation to the capacity of men to love all of their Christian brothers with the time they personally spend with God and meditate on His Word. The less time you spend with God, the higher the degree of certainty that you will find yourself despising or denigrating another Christian brother in your heart (even if you don't say it out loud, God knows your heart). This is not to rebuke anyone, and I state this as a matter of fact, just as I would advise a brother to drink more water when they are clearly dehydrated.

In verses 1:24-25, Peter is quoting from Isaiah 40:6-8, which declares that our human life is a transition into something more, but only a spiritual life that is sprouted from the Word of God will be forever under His embrace. Peter concludes his quote from Isaiah with an affirmation that the Word was preached for you and me and merges the New Gospel message with Isaiah's Old Testament reference to the Word of God[25]. It also serves to compare and contrast the weakness of our flesh with the power of God's Word.

As brothers in Christ, our new life can't move forward unless we repent and all our sins are confessed and forgiven (at least the ones we can recall, remember, or be convicted of). When this happens, this is when the Word of God begins to operate in our lives. Most translations refer to ridding ourselves of *"evil behavior,"* which Peter states in verse 2:1. The type of evil referenced in this passage is the type exhibited by a person and is not the same as the type committed by satan.[26]

The King James Version writes 2:2 like this: *"As newborn babes, desire the sincere milk of the Word, that ye may grow …"* Many scholars believe that 1 Peter chapter 1 should continue through to verse 2:3 [27] because the subject matter continues with the material that began back in 1:22, as indicated by the word *"Therefore"* in verse 2:1. The NLT for verse 2:1, as used in the Chapter of this book, begins with the word *"So,"* while other translations use the word *"Therefore."* Nonetheless, Peter continues to plead with his readers that they remain focused on the impact of their rebirth.

Peter is admonishing us to get rid of everything that is considered *"evil behavior"* (malice, guile, deceit, hypocrisy, envy, slander). I don't believe this list is exhaustive, meaning that Peter wasn't picking on just these sinful behaviors, but could have continued with more evil characteristics (i.e., lust, gossip, greed, etc.). However, it is notable that the sins Peter does list out are those that tend to cause the greatest disruption of fellowship within the Church and, as a result, prevent the Church from completing its part in a believer's growth. [28] The impact is that the Church becomes distracted.

- Malice is a belligerent attitude toward another believer, usually for selfish reasons.
- Guile is a desire to trick someone.
- Hypocrisy is pretending to be something one is not, and envy is wishing to be like someone or have something someone has.
- Slander is a misrepresentation of another to his or her detriment (an extreme form of gossip).

Peter is telling us in verse 2:2 that we ought to behave like newborn babies, who desire milk over solid food, so that we can grow and mature in respect to our new life in Christ after we are born again. We are all immature in our faith after our initial justification and we gravitate towards solid food (meaning areas that are more complex from a spiritual perspective) as our spiritual maturity can handle it. Our spiritual maturity increases as our hunger for God's Word becomes intense and insatiable.[29] Milk is a reference to spiritual items that are more foundational to our faith; but as we mature in the faith, we need something that is more filling, nourishing, and strengthening.

This progression of spiritual intensity is a normal sign of a genuine conversion. If a brother isn't getting to this level, and continues to lack this type of hunger, this is a possible sign of spiritual indifference or spiritual apathy. This is the brother who will also find that he is struggling to love all of his Christian brothers as alluded to earlier. He very likely loves Jesus (or perhaps the thought of Jesus) but something is keeping him from going "all in." The brother may not even know why, but he will likely realize that something is off on his own and conclude that he requires spiritual coaching and mentorship to move forward. What is hard for him, in this case, is being humble and mustering the courage to seek out that coaching.

A brother's desire for the truth of both Christ and God's Word develops and increases as he matures. Simultaneously, the brother should find that he has virtually eliminated sin from his life, that his ability in openly admitting his desire and need for God's truth grows, that his pursuit of spiritual growth increases[30], and that he has learned to automatically see and appreciate the blessings in his life (rather than intentionally having to focus to see them).

In verse 2:3, "*...now that you have had a taste of the Lord's kindness*," Peter is touching upon a verse from Psalm 34:8:

> *Psalm 34:8: "Taste and see that the Lord is good. How happy is the person who takes refuge in Him!"*

Peter furthers this concept of fervent hunger for God's truth and Word by telling the reader that you can successfully remove sin from your life and that you will experience an insatiable hunger if you, the believer, are being honest with yourself and others that you have truly experienced the graciousness of God. If you can't recognize His grace or admit that it was His grace that you have experienced, you may experience an obstruction to your spiritual growth as you are likely placing credit on yourself.

If you have truly experienced God, then that is all that is necessary for you to move towards spiritual maturity – beyond milk and to solid food. Newborn babies require adults to take care of them and teach them. In a spiritual sense, all newborn believers need to latch on to the faith of others to begin their new walk with Christ. However, a time should come when believers no longer requires the faith of others and can progress independently on their own faith. This does not mean that we don't need spiritual advisors and brothers in our lives – we do. Even the disciples and apostles always moved in groups of two or more. However, if, after a period of time, we find that we are still dependent on the faith of others, then we are not maturing in Christ as we should. If you've been in this state for a few years, it may be time to examine yourself, humbly speak with another brother, and find where you are lacking. By doing this action, you are indirectly, and fervently, seeking the things of God in your life. Praise God!

5

The Living Stone and a Chosen People
1 Peter 2:4 - 12 (CSB)

PREMISE

The Lord Jesus is described as a Living Stone who is precious in God's sight – the corner stone, the rejected stone, and the stone that will be stumbled over. Believers are also seen as living stones who are to be built up as part of a spiritual house to carry out a holy priesthood (the Church). Peter shows the reader where Christ fulfilled several Old Testament prophecies as God's choice stone and as a rock of offense before an unbelieving world that sees the Gospel as offensive. Peter counsels believers to live godly lives, no matter what, glorifying God until the day He returns. [1]

First Peter Chapter 2 (cont'd)

[4] As you come to him, a living stone—rejected by people but chosen and honored by God— [5] you yourselves, as living stones, a spiritual house, are being built to be a holy priesthood to offer spiritual sacrifices acceptable to God through Jesus Christ. [6] For it stands in Scripture:

> *See, I lay a stone in Zion,*
> *a chosen and honored cornerstone,*
> *and the one who believes in him*
> *will never be put to shame.*

[7] So honor will come to you who believe; but for the unbelieving,

> *The stone that the builders rejected—*
> *this one has become the cornerstone,*

[8] and

> *A stone to stumble over,*
> *and a rock to trip over.*

They stumble because they disobey the word; they were destined for this.

[9] But you are a chosen race, a royal priesthood, a holy nation, a people for his possession, so that you may proclaim the praises of the one who called you out of darkness into his marvelous light. [10] Once you were not a people, but now you are God's people; you had not received mercy, but now you have received mercy.

[11] Dear friends, I urge you as strangers and exiles to abstain from sinful desires that wage war against the soul. [12] Conduct yourselves honorably among the Gentiles, so that when they slander you as evildoers, they will observe your good works and will glorify God on the day he visits.

The Living Stone and a Chosen People

When Christians say that they are "coming to Jesus," they are declaring that they intend to remain firmly established in a relationship with Him as part of their daily fellowship with Him. Coming to Him means that we intend to remain in His presence, not just some of the time or whenever we want.

As Peter opens this new section of his letter, he recognizes that, just as Jesus was rejected, so are believers who "come to Him" because of their faith: you will likely be mocked, scorned, or simply rejected and ignored. Persecution isn't always physical; sometimes it's emotional. To be rejected or ignored implies that society doesn't want anything to do with you, which can hurt more for those that are striving for relevancy. But, if we recognize that even Jesus, the greatest person who ever lived, was rejected, then our own personal rejection is easier to deal with. And, as the world knows, Jesus was, and is, extremely relevant.

When we come to Jesus, we come to Him as living stones, people who are precious in the eyes of the Lord[2]. The use of the word "stone" is a common image throughout scripture, usually referring to building up in a spiritual sense, just like a physical building. It is Jesus, the Living Stone that serves as the foundation of our faith and our spirituality. Without Him, the entire spiritual building collapses – and our faith crashes.

Jesus as the Living Stone is a paradox both in Old Testament scriptures[3] as well as in 1 Peter 2:6-8. Peter is emphasizing that Jesus is alive and has a real relationship with believers, but he also points to the calamity that unbelievers will ultimately suffer.

Christ's rejection was prophesied in the Old Testament, but His rejection led to something new and beautiful – His Church[4]. As the Living Stone, Jesus is alive; He is not dead. We, as living stones as Peter says in 2:5, are being built up as a spiritual household[5]. This is also part of a holy priesthood, where we are to offer up what is referred to as "spiritual sacrifices" acceptable to God[6]. Such sacrifices reach God through Jesus Christ as He reminds us in John 14:6 ("*nobody gets to the Father except through Me*"). Some translations say, "*into a temple of the Spirit*" in lieu of" into *a spiritual house.*"

John McArthur wrote that "building a spiritual house means putting all believers in place, integrating each one with others, and each one with the life of Christ."[7] Since the components that make up this spiritual house are living, this implies that the house is growing. But, unlike traditional churches, His Church doesn't have a formal priesthood[8]: His Church **IS** a priesthood – the entire Church, meaning you and me. We are the priesthood that makes up His Church.

As members of the holy priesthood, our lives should be so closely identified and united with Christ that the very life of Christ flows through our veins. And, as members of the priesthood, we all share a number of privileges but the most exciting and awesome privilege of a priest is that we have direct access to God.[9]

- Priesthood is an elect privilege.
- Priests are cleansed of sins.
- Priests are clothed for service.
- Priests are anointed for service.

- Priests are prepared for service.
- Priests are ordained to obedience.
- Priests are to honor the word of God.
- Priests are to walk with God.
- Priests are to impact sinners.
- Priests are messengers of God.

The sacrifice that is acceptable to God through Jesus Christ is identified in 2:5. This sacrifice is the ministry that you perform as you exercise your spiritual gift(s). Your ministry is one that God honors because of Christ, because you are doing it under the direction and guidance of the Holy Spirit, and because it follows the Word of God. As outlined in the NASB Study Bible, your duties might include:

- Offering your strength as a part of the body of God
- Praising God
- Doing good
- Sharing your resources
- Bringing people to Christ
- Sacrificing your desires for the good of others
- Praying
- and more

Sometimes our duties will involve mediating between God and the world as we take our missions (or ministries) to the world. In 2:6, Peter was quoting from Isaiah 28:16: "*So this is what the Sovereign Lord says: 'See, I lay a stone in Zion, a tested stone, a precious cornerstone for a sure foundation; the one who relies on it will never be stricken with panic.'*" This quote refers to a Messiah who is the cornerstone in whom we can believe and will never be disappointed.[10]

Peter is identifying Jesus as the Messiah who God honored when He rose Him from the dead; and those who put their trust in Him will be vindicated and validated in the last days. The cornerstone reference in 2:7 refers to Jesus and His leadership role in the Church, a quote that Peter pulled from Psalm 118:22 *"The stone the builders rejected has become the chief cornerstone..."*

This quote refers to Jesus, who came to save the nation, having been rejected by the Jewish leaders and influencers who were responsible for building the nation of Israel. Peter is using this verse to inform us that these unbelieving builders also played their part in seeing the prophecy fulfilled by rejecting Jesus.

In 2:8, Peter is quoting from Isaiah 8:14, *"He will be a holy place; for both Israel and Judah he will be a stone that causes people to stumble and a rock that makes them fall. And for the people of Jerusalem he will be a trap and a snare."* This refers to Jesus and how He will cause the Jews to stumble over the truth, and how they will refuse to obey His message of repentance and faith[11]. Peter is telling us that those who reject the stone will stumble over it because they are offended by it: the very stone God established has become the means of their falling.

> *"The word skandalon is used to describe how unbelievers react to the Gospel when they don't want to hear it or believe it. Peter said, 'And a stone of stumbling, and a rock of offence, even to them which stumble at the word...' Rather than accept the message and be saved, these people stumble when they hear the truth, tripping over the message that could set them free."* ~ Rick Renner[12]

In verses 2:6-8, Peter continues with a series of prophetic quotations from the Old Testament. This is a wonderful example of why the Old Testament is relevant to the modern Christian as the backbone of the New Testament. These three verses reveal that Jesus is the living stone, the cornerstone, the rejected stone, and the stone that will be stumbled over.

It's in verse 8 where Peter concludes his stone metaphor by explaining that those who stumble over the stone will do so because they are being disobedient to the word. It wasn't the stone's appearance, nor was it Jesus that offended them: it was the message He was preaching that they rejected. It was, and still is, an unwelcome message to those who are living a depraved life because it points to their depravity. It challenges unbelievers to confront the way they are living, and they don't like it because it involves telling them how they ought to and ought not to live. Ironically, the public will generally follow all secular and man-made laws, even to the detriment of their own liberty or freedom but mention biblical laws, even those that run parallel to secular laws, and unbelievers will reject them. The challenges for unbelievers typically revolve around moral standards of behavior and conduct that are expected from "Someone" they fail to see; they add to the crisis by deciding to actually refuse to see Him, they don't want to see Him.

The most ominous statement Peter makes in v.8 is that those who stumble are doomed to meet the fate planned for them[13], implying the obvious – that more than one person will disobey and not everyone will be saved. Verse 8 is one of several verses used as evidence by those who believe in the Doctrine of Reprobation.

Reprobation[14] is a theology that teaches that a person can reject the Gospel to the point that God will eventually give up on them and reject them, and then He curses them to sin. However, I, for one, don't believe this doctrine because it is contrary to *who* God is. God will never reject a person, no matter what they do, but, if they reject God, then they will pay the ultimate price for that rejection – they will meet their fate.

This verse is also used by those who believe in the Doctrine of Predestination (previously outlined in Chapter 3)[15]. Believers of this theology believe that everyone was born into a destiny and predestined at birth to either go to heaven or hell. There are plenty of scriptures that refer to foreknowledge and destiny; but, while God may know ahead of time where a person will end up, He affords the opportunity to everyone to make their own choices. God has predestined, not who will disobey, but only what the result of disobedience will be for those who persist in disobedience.

Now, just because He knew a person would reject Him does not mean that God created the person for the purpose of rejecting Him. This is just absurd on its merits as it would imply that God creates people for the purpose of sending them to hell. The truth is, a person is doomed to go to hell because of the choices that they made – their decisions. It is their fault because of their refusal to obey the Gospel – it is not God's fault.

Thus, for all of us, Christ can either be the means of their salvation (if they choose to believe), or their means of judgment (if they reject Him). The judgment a person will receive because of their unbelief is fulfilled the exact same way a person receives salvation by their faith.

As Peter begins to allude to in 2:9, Christ fully expects that His followers will live a holy lifestyle and rely on Spirit-led common sense to move away from the proverbial cliff. Why wouldn't He? He was the One that called us out of our darkness into His light and He knew that skirting the cliff, a metaphor for the playing around the edges of sin, is not the way to flourish. This means that we need to be careful about placing ourselves into positions where we allow sinful pleasures to tease us or tempt us.

If you have a history of alcohol abuse, stay away from bars. Don't even drink a beer if your alcohol abuse was related to hard liquor. If you have a history of pornography, stay away from media and entertainment that borders on porn. Even movies that only contain brief nude scenes can be skirting the edge of the cliff. This is what the Holy Spirit was pleading through Peter. In verse 2:9, in contrast to the fate of unbelievers, Peter is moving on to those who are obedient, that is, the elect of Christ. When Peter was referring to believers as a chosen race, a royal priesthood, a holy nation, and God's people, he is comparing Christ followers and the Church to the nation of Israel[16], as drawn from Exodus 19:6.

Exodus 19:6: "'and you will be my kingdom of priests and my holy nation.' These are the words that you are to say to the Israelites."

While there are similarities between Israel and the Church (which is preached on often enough), there are also dissimilarities[17].

However, I believe it is fair to classify the Church as a chosen race of new and special people. A Jew will always be a Jew and a Gentile will always be a Gentile, but they can both be one new people from the two groups (Ephesians 2:15), and while all believers are priests, they are not part of a particular tribe. When comparing the Church with nations, while the Church is a holy nation, the nations of the planet are something less then holy; and the Church is not a political party (at least, it's not supposed to be).

It may be hard for some (even though it shouldn't be), but all believers are supposed to represent God and His Word all of the time, declaring through the Word and their lifestyles that God knows how people need to live in the world. Unfortunately, Israel temporarily forfeited its right as a royal priesthood when the nation rejected Jesus Christ (at least, until Israel accepts Him as the Messiah, see Isaiah 6:9-13). Paul adds in Romans 11:25-26 that Israel has been partially hardened *"until the fullness of the Gentiles has come in; and so all Israel will be saved;..."* We, as believers today, need to avoid the mistakes that Israel made.

It is because of God's grace that some come to have faith and, as God's elect, we are to be proclaiming everything about Him[18] because He was the One who delivered us from that pit of darkness. In 2:10, Peter quotes from Hosea that you were once *"not a people"* but *"now you are the people of God."*

> *Hosea 1:10; 2:23: "Yet the number of the Israelites will be like the sand of the sea, which cannot be measured or counted. And in the place where they were told: You are not my people, they will be called: Sons of the living*

God…. I will sow her in the land for myself, and I will have compassion on Lo-ruhamah; I will say to Lo-ammi: You are my people, and he will say, 'You are my God.'"

Peter then continues with the warning that, while Christians are the people of God and have received His mercy, they may actually suffer for that very reason, but the suffering is worth it. What? Yes, you read that correctly.

For the people that he was writing to, Peter was reminding them that it was the moment they heard the message of redemption, due to God's mercy, that they became God's people. Peter was also making a reference to Israel as they will, one day, be part of the Church of Jesus Christ. The prophet Hosea promised that Israel, though remaining outside of God's blessing for a long period of time, would eventually come back under God's mercy. God's dealing with Israel is a similar pattern for how He is dealing with believers today under the New Covenant; those who previously were outside of God's covenant but are now under the mercy of God by faith in Christ (see Romans 11:2).

The Christian Life is both a Battle AND a Witness

Verse 2:11 is the beginning of a new train of thought in Peter's letter. Peter is again reminding us that, as Christians, we are foreigners in a secular society because our citizenship is in heaven. While we are on earth, we need to choose how to view our life: 1) as strangers, 2) as citizens, or 3) as servants[19]. Christ Himself sets the example by showing how He led a perfect life right in the middle of all of the chaos and hostility while He walked the earth – as a servant. If He did it, then we can do it as well.

For many believers, it seems that we have those one or two very particular temptations that we fight much more frequently than others. We live for Jesus, and we want to please Him, at least we should want to; however, the vast majority of us live and work in environments where the temptations of sin beat on us relentlessly. In these environments, it's admittedly difficult to abstain from certain activities, pleasures, and temptations that go against our new life; it is arguably more difficult for those that come to Christ later in life. It's really easy to get drawn back into our older lifestyles when we never fully separate from parts of that life that we enjoy too much, even though we know that Christ would not approve.

Peter knew that for the audience he was writing for, the societies in which they lived openly celebrated sin and flaunted it in front of everyone (including the children). If what they were celebrating is in sync with your old life, the struggle becomes that much more real and complicated. It can make you feel isolated, that you're being left out, and it hurts because you want to jump back into something you used to do feeling at the same time conflicted because you know that it goes against your new life.

Some men also find pleasure in cynicism, fighting, and sarcasm – which is not Christ-like. Other men find pleasure in alcohol, drugs, or sexual immorality. It's hard and the temptation is strong, which is why Peter states that it's like *war against your soul.* But, on the other hand, we do have a code of discipline which should be reflected in our private lives, and not just when people can see us.

In 2:11, Peter is urging us to remain in the righteous life; it's too easy to give into worldly temptations. Paul writes all about these struggles in Romans Chapter 7. The Greek word Peter used for *urge* (or *beseech* in other translations) was *parakaleo*, which is also a military word expressing a sense of urgency in times of war. By using this word, it is possible that many believers he was writing to may have looked to Peter as a General of the faith. This is interesting because Peter did refer to temptations as a *war* against your soul.

War draws a picture of soldiers in combat, and for some men the lure of temptation is so strong that it is a literal war in their mind and soul. If we ever give in and let our flesh have what it wants, the battle against succumbing to it or similar temptations in the future becomes ferocious and gets stronger and stronger. This is why Peter was beseeching us never to indulge but to always, completely, abstain. Don't think that to participate, even just a little, you can just walk free from it.

For some men in particular, the urge is so strong that they can feel their tension rise, their body shake, and sometimes tears will well up in their eyes because they REALLY want to do "that one thing." But they also know that it's not consistent with Christ. It is a very real battle, one that can actually cause physical problems in the man whether he gives in to the temptation or not (usually joint- or heart-related). It's as if you are up against an army of rebels or guerillas who are constantly harassing you in an attempt to destroy your supply lines and your morale. In this case, your lines reach to God who supplies you with the spiritual fruit of joy and peace.

Sadly, some men cave into the pressure; but if you are one that did cave, don't condemn yourself, repent and get back on track. The Lord forgives you, but you must truly repent. Saying "sorry" isn't good enough, particularly if you don't feel any remorse for what you did (or what you said) and you know you will do it again. That is not repentance. Repentance is willing to turn away completely from that sin.

As Peter concludes this section of the letter in verse 2:12, he is admonishing believers to live rightly and honorably, no matter what others are saying to you or about you, or what they may be doing to you or around you. It is by your example that those operating maliciously around you will see how you react and how you continue to glorify God, no matter what. This is it; this is the summation of what a relationship with Jesus Christ is about. How we relate with those that are rejecting Him says a lot about that relationship. The Christian must outwardly live among non-Christians in a way that reflects their inward discipline.

We are living in a world where there are many who don't have the same values or belief system, so we should fully expect to be treated differently by such people. Some will be more antagonistic than others; some will simply avoid and ignore you or your belief system by isolating you (they will never invite you to anything again). I have family members that roll their eyes every time I pray – and that's okay. Bottom line is that the world is a hostile place and, as believers, we are to turn away from the sinful desires that once held us in bondage. And we should not cave into the pressure.

We are not only to live our lives by godly morals, but we are always to be respectful, kind, and friendly to others – oh boy, this is a really tough one in today's political and cultural climate. In fact, it is the type of climate we are experiencing in 2021 where many men fall, declaring, "Screw it!" and cave to what their flesh wants to do. But people notice your conduct. Did you know that if you live a respectful, kind, and friendly way towards non-believers, this witness to them may be the basis on which their lives turn around? It might take years, but your behavior can be that which gives people hope: when they see no hope at all, they will want what you have. Can you imagine what God will say to you if you choose to live by His pattern on the day that He finally visits us (on His return)?

This doesn't mean that we live our life as robots or as door mats – but that is a discussion for another day. Peter was teaching that, when the grace of God visits the heart of an unbeliever, the unbeliever may someday respond with saving faith and openly glorify God because he remembers the testimony of believers he had observed. I know this is the truth because it is a part of my own testimony.

6

Submission to Authority and A Call to Good Works
1 Peter 2:13 - 17 (ESV)

PREMISE

We are entering into an area of Peter's letter where he begins a deep dive into the topic of submission – submission even during times of persecution and slander. When believers submit to "legitimate" human authority, they are operating according to the will of God, which serves as a witness that can silence ignorant and foolish men (a reference to Gentiles and those doing the persecuting and slandering).[1]

Believers are not to use their freedom of salvation to cover up any sinful acts they may commit (in other words, just because you are saved does not give you a right to sin). Salvation is not a "get out-of-

jail-free card." Believers are connected with God, spirit to Spirit, and we are supposed to honor men, love our brothers, and honor Him as King.

Peter may, or may not, have suspected that there would be a severe uprising in Rome a few years after he wrote this letter that would turn against Christ followers. Nonetheless, when governments act up, it's easy for believers to view government authority with contempt and bitterness, and when we do this, we will, in the end, violate our testimony. Paul made a similar statement in Romans 13:1 where he explicitly states that there is no authority except that which is from God and those in positions of "legitimate" authority are established by God. However, some men strive to implement their own authority that is contrary to God's Word and God's standards of morality. The principle being stated here is that believers must respect God honored authority even when it seems that that authority is abused.[2] However, authority that does not honor God or respect His standards of morality and conduct should be rejected...with grace. And this right here is where many Christian men lose it (myself included)

Just take a look around the American nation today (2021) – the government is rampant with abuse across all parties (abuse is non-partisan) and it is rare to find anyone that will disagree that abuse is happening. Where we differ is on what is considered or defined as "abuse," as this is where our personal opinion and other factors come into play. However, the definition of abuse of authority and what to do about it is not discussed in 1 Peter nor the passage in Romans chapter 13. For that, we need to go elsewhere in scripture.

In Acts 4, the governing authorities restricted Christians from preaching the Gospel. This is when, according to both Peter and Paul, believers must obey God over men, for God's laws and man's laws are in conflict. When we do this, there are other scriptures that outline, or show by example, how believers do this. We must behave and conduct ourselves as citizens and free people of God's Kingdom, and this means that we always do things that honor Him.[3]

First Peter Chapter 2 (cont'd)

[13] Be subject for the Lord's sake to every human institution, whether it be to the emperor as supreme, [14] or to governors as sent by him to punish those who do evil and to praise those who do good. [15] For this is the will of God, that by doing good you should put to silence the ignorance of foolish people. [16] Live as people who are free, not using your freedom as a cover-up for evil, but living as servants of God. [17] Honor everyone. Love the brotherhood. Fear God. Honor the emperor.

Submission to Authority and a Call to Good Works

The idea of submission in verse 2:13 is written somewhat within the context of a ranking system, similar to the military rank structure where everyone is always ranked under someone. This idea of submission is placing yourself in an attitude of submission to that authority placed over you in a humble way, even while in the midst of a godless and slanderous society. Even though believers are citizens of heaven, Peter is telling us that it is God's will that we remain obedient to those people placed in positions of authority in the world. Doing this honors God and anything contrary to this, such as living in a state of rebellion, dishonors Christ.

In verses 2:13-14, Peter is concerned that the readers of his letter maintain a godly stance towards people in authority so that they can continue to maintain a godly testimony in front of all people, primarily unbelievers.[4] Our submission to authority is something Peter advises that is crucial for the welfare of our salvation. This is admittedly very difficult to do when you are living under the authority of officials who hold political, cultural, or social views that are not only in opposition to God and Christian views, but polarizing.

Submission is something we do for God for His sake and His honor; since the world sees and views God through the witness of believers (like us).[5] This makes sense, although it may make some nervous (because we tend to focus more on imperfections than on God's grace upon our life). When we behave in a jaded and bitter way, when we lash out at others, and then, somewhere in our communication pattern we declare our love for God and church as well as our biblical values, people will view God in exactly that way — right or wrong, that is what they do. I did that and many of you do, or did, as well. The premise is that this sort of behavior embarrasses God and dishonors Jesus. It's not about "What Would Jesus Do?" It's more about "What Did Jesus Do?". Jesus not only shared his ministry of love, healing, and compassion; however, He also threw out corrupt traders and sellers from the temple because they had defiled the sanctity of His House (see Matthew 21:12-13).

Submission to authority includes submitting to government (particularly officials that have been legitimately placed in political office). In principle, I believe in the paradigm that the fundamental purpose of government is to deter evil, punish evildoers, and praise and reward those who do right, which encourages more good behavior; all of which is based on biblical principles and morals.[6] Paul stated as such in Romans 13:3-5, where he declared that civil authorities are supposed to be ministers of God for good and avengers who bring wrath to those who do evil.

I have stated a few times about submission to legitimate members of government (i.e., authority); this implies that I believe there are members of government and authority who are not legitimate, meaning that they were not placed there by God but achieved their position via evil, malicious, and sinful ways. Whether legitimacy can be proven or not, you can see who these people are based on their view of the role of government and whether they minister, either implicitly or explicitly, Spirit induced Godly morals and values.

The biblical ideal is to constrain government to areas of protection and justice, along with the areas that are ancillary to them (such as collecting taxes). Anything that reaches beyond this constraint does not fit the model of government that God outlines in scripture. It is His Church that is supposed to pick up and run with those operations that fall outside of the biblical ideals of government, such as education, healthcare, et cetera. Within the United States, nowhere within the US Constitution does it mention anything resembling federal government oversight of healthcare or education.

Yet, the people have accepted the governments legislative role into these areas, amongst others, which not only violates the US Constitution, but more importantly, it does not meet God's outline for government found within scripture either; perhaps this is why the Founders did not include them. The United States is not unique in this regard.

Making matters more challenging, our modern world is actively turning government bodies into enforcers of socialistic welfare; when this happens, we lose more and more of our liberty. As we lose more of our liberty, we slowly transition into a system of full on socialism, which consistently, every time, morphs into totalitarianism if it is not confronted. History proves this. The morphing from socialism to totalitarianism happens gradually as people become accustomed to government control, and then the people both accept and expect government to be the dominant provider and the agency who tells us what to do about anything and everything.

Men weaken as a result, slowly giving up their masculinity, and when this happens, God's people become weakened to the point that they "want" government to provide and to tell them what to do about anything and everything, while completely neglecting God's promises, His commands, and His provision. This is not the same thing as submission. This is both weak and slothful, and I firmly believe is contrary to the Word of God and is sinful. When we place our dependence on man and not on God, we are being disobedient to God and are then living in sin. When we allow, or even demand, men to govern areas of our lives contrary to God's expectations for living and liberty, we are being disobedient to what God offers and, as a result, find ourselves living outside His will.

When man is mandating morality and morality is not in accordance with God's standards of living, then as believers we are fully expected to live God's way over man's way. I believe this is when we should not submit, humbly and without pride or ego, and we are never to dishonor God. Everything we do should be justified and supported in Scripture – the way He wrote it, not the way we prefer to interpret it. We are to live as men the way God designed us to live as men. This is where we can see the hope that He has for us. It is both acceptable and expected that men of God confront abuse of authority through political means and legal forms of activism if necessary; however, while we are all created in the image of God, the men that undertake these types of activities must ensure they are following the will of God for their lives and they are properly equipped to execute God's plan. In this regard, we are not ALL created equal when it comes to skills and talents. Passion or dissatisfaction is not enough and can make you act foolish while leading you to sin and disobedience if not careful.

Nonetheless, no matter what we do and how hard we try, it has already been ordained and prophesied within Scripture that government will trend towards the Anti-Christ system (which includes large government).[7] Therefore, any reprieves we receive in limited government are only going to be temporary. And it is also true to say that there are members of the "Institutionalized" Church who are, and will be complicit, knowingly or unknowingly, in bringing unbiblical government into service. As we keep this in the forefront of our minds, it should reduce anxiety and stress, and prevent opportunities to backslide over the proverbial cliff discussed in the previous chapter. Ironically, it is the Church as an organism (the communion of believers) that will see this happening as it happens, and where the core of influencers who will speak out against this form of government will flow. Refer back to chapter 5 where we discuss the topic of Jesus Christ as the Living Stone and how the members of His Church are all living stones who are His priesthood (the Church as an organism).

Peter concludes this thought in 2:15 by reminding us that when we do right [by God], which means living according to His Word, this silences the ignorance of fools. One of the unfortunate things that happened to First Century Christ followers is that they became characterized as anarchists because they claimed their citizenship was in heaven and not in the nation they were living.[8] Although it is true, they had the Word to back up their claim, this did not imply disobedience to the State, as misconstrued by unbelievers. This is why, and when, unbelievers started retaliating against these early Christians, something that continues to this very day, and feels somewhat similar to the experiences of many believers in the 21st Century.

By doing good and continuing to be aligned with God's will for us, this does not mean that we will avoid any kind of persecution. What believers need to focus on is to avoid condemnation while winning commendation. Most of the time, our consistent walk with God will actually shut the mouths of those who are against the faith and are looking for every reason they can to criticize us. For, just like executives in large corporations, or high-ranking military officers, and senior political officials, everything we say and do is, and will be, measured and judged by unbelievers, or they shut you out of their lives through isolation as much as they possibly can. In some cases, this might be acceptable and met with approval by all concerned (though I believe this is contrary to God's standards of living).

As pointed out by Peter in 2:16, as we silence the ignorance of foolish men, we do this as free men, but we should not misuse our freedom (our salvation via God's grace) as a cover up for evil. Covering for evil implies that you are misleading people into thinking that your activities are good, when they are motivated by selfish reasons.[9] Again, being free men means that we are doing good and living our lives based on decisions following the will of God and not based on some forced compulsion or false pretense to please men.

Your freedom in Christ does not give you license to sin or self-indulge, rather, it is based on your devotion to do what is good in the eyes of God.

> Galatians 5:13-14: "You, my brothers and sisters, were called to be free. But do not use your freedom to indulge the flesh; rather, serve one another humbly in love. For the entire law is fulfilled in keeping this one command: 'Love your neighbor as yourself.'"

We need to enjoy our freedom but not do it with a veil or mask. Be real and remain true; this is what Peter is warning us about.

Peter concludes this section of his letter in 2:17 by expanding on the idea of submission based on the premise that we are to honor and respect all men.[10] Meditate on that a bit. We live in a culture today filled with anger, bitterness, offense, and other negative emotions. These negative emotions will mask the positive emotions of love, respect, and honor, among others. Negative emotions get more publicity, and this has, unfortunately, taught those that need or want attention to behave in a negative manner. Of course, even this only goes so far.

To be more specific, no matter what the world is doing, we are commanded by God to love the Christian brotherhood. The quality of our love should be higher for our Christian brothers than for unbelievers, but we honor God and exhort Him as King by loving even unbelievers.[11] If your instinctive reaction to this statement was to roll your eyes, or your heart to beat a little faster, or if you smirked, you are not alone. Our global climate makes this idea of love one of the greatest challenges we have today, above anything. But the idea of loving our brothers, and others, is not just an obedient duty, but something that we need to try and develop as an inward sense of respect as well. This is the kind of love that feeds your faith and gives one HOPE as discussed in chapter 3.

And remember, love is an act, not an emotion. This act tends to change the context for some when we view love properly. Anyone can say they love people, but many may not show that love by their actions.

7

The Kind of Life Jesus Lived, The Relevance of Christ as Our Example
1 Peter 2:18 - 25 (MSG)

PREMISE

Peter talks about servants' submission to their masters, even to those who are unjust/unfair/prejudiced/inappropriate, et cetera. The belief is that by our very act of submission, we will find favor with God. This belief is based on the idea that Christians are to follow the example set by Jesus and walk in His steps, meaning we do what He did. When He was walking the earth, Jesus was reviled and ridiculed, but, He never responded in kind to what those who messed with Him did. In fact, Christ went so far as to die on the cross for all of us, including the same ones who reviled and ridiculed Him (and those that would do the same thing over the millennia that followed). Jesus is now the Shepherd and Guardian of our souls and it was by His death and His wounds that we are healed. [1]

First Peter Chapter 2 (cont'd)

[18-20] You who are servants, be good servants to your masters—not just to good masters, but also to bad ones. What counts is that you put up with it for God's sake when you're treated badly for no good reason. There's no particular virtue in accepting punishment that you well deserve. But if you're treated badly for good behavior and continue in spite of it to be a good servant, that is what counts with God.

[21-25] This is the kind of life you've been invited into, the kind of life Christ lived. He suffered everything that came his way so you would know that it could be done, and also know how to do it, step-by-step.

He never did one thing wrong,
Not once said anything amiss.

They called him every name in the book and he said nothing back. He suffered in silence, content to let God set things right. He used his servant body to carry our sins to the Cross so we could be rid of sin, free to live the right way. His wounds became your healing. You were lost sheep with no idea who you were or where you were going. Now you're named and kept for good by the Shepherd of your souls.

The Kind of Life Jesus Lived and His Relevance as Our Example

This section opens in verse 2:18 by immediately making a reference to "servants," but some interpret this word as slaves (the NIV and NLT, for example). In the original Greek, Peter used the word *oiketes,* which is translated "servants," so I am not sure where these other translations are getting the idea of slaves. A servant is someone who has a boss that they work for and answer to; it is not a reference to a person who is considered or classified as property. More specifically, many bible scholars believe, as do I, that Peter was making a specific reference to a "household servant" – a domestic, a butler, or a maid, for example. Peter follows in this verse by calling on "servants" to be subject to their "masters." Oh boy!

The word "masters" is another word that many associate with someone who is literally over slaves. In the original Greek, Peter used the word *despotes*, which refers to a person who is of supreme authority in his household (or head of the family). In this verse, I believe that Peter is referring to all of those who are in positions of authority over servants, not in the sense of a master-slave relationship, but in the sense of management, supervision, and authority. A husband, for example, is master of his house (this is NOT a jab at feminists). In contrast, if you check out Ephesians 6:5-9, you will read where Paul is advising slaves – *douloi* (translated accurately) – to be obedient to their masters.

Some commentary and bible studies will delve deeper into this verse on the topic of slavery, comparing and contrasting the concept of slavery in the First Century Mediterranean with slavery in pre-Civil War America.[2] This verse has been used by modern day secularists and progressives to somehow prove that American Christians are responsible for the invention of slavery. While America did, unfortunately, continue with the practice of slavery both before and after its founding, America did not create slavery; yet this does not stop others from placing this evil trade on the shoulders of America. As the word in this verse (*oiketes*) is more accurately translated as servant, I am not sure commentary from this area of scripture on the topic of slavery is an appropriate fit while it may be appropriate in other verses where the word for slave is translated literally.

In either case, and to get back on point, it is a fact that there are "masters," or people in authority, who can be kind, but there are also those who can be cruel or harsh. Regardless, Peter is advising believers to submit to all those in positions of authority, not only those that are awesome, but also those who are the polar opposite. This is something that those of us who may have rough and tough Type A characteristics may not accept, but if we truly consider the Word of God as absolute, then it is our responsibility to simply obey Him. So, why is Peter giving us this difficult advice? Why is Peter telling is that we are to submit "in all respect" (in reverent fear) whether the master is good or "unreasonable"?

Verse 2:19 clarifies this. "What counts" (MSG) / "Commendable" (NKJV) /"This finds favor" (NASB)/"This is a gracious thing" (ESV) – implies that believers who patiently endure suffering are, in effect, proof (or evidence) of God's grace at work. Verse 2:20

continues with the assurance that God's people will find a reward from Him if they endure suffering righteously. Along with His grace will come His favor and blessing in due time. We are to live with "patient endurance."[3] Ugh!

Being conscious of God implies our obligation towards Him, meaning that we are to keep our minds steadfastly on God (Isaiah 26:3). He did save us from a life of eternal damnation, right?

"Credit" (as used in the NASB) implies glory. The MSG paraphrase for verse 20 used in this chapter of this book states that "there is no particular virtue in accepting punishment that you well deserve." Peter says the reason for this is because you actually did something that earned that punishment – a monetary fine or perhaps being fired from the job. However, if you suffer or endure a punishment for doing good (implying that the punishment is not deserved), then this is something that is commendable in God's eyes.

Let's be honest, being punished unjustly would cause anyone to seethe with anger, be irate and extremely frustrated. You may sense an almost overwhelming urge to rebel and fight, or retaliate as soon as the opportunity arose. There are "masters" out there who would expect you to retaliate; they want you to respond negatively in some fashion, and they look forward to it so that they can punish you more for it – to continue your suffering.[4] However, not retaliating is something that might catch their attention and make them curious. As we will see later in verse 3:15, you may even cause this person to ask you to share why you still have hope when they think you should feel hopeless.

Beginning in verse 2:21 and carried through to verse 2:25, Peter is explaining to his readers that it is more than appropriate for us to follow the example of Jesus Christ, who Himself suffered unjustly for the world. It's easy for anyone to accept a call to salvation or to ministry, but toss in suffering or the need to accept suffering, and we either miss that part or misunderstand it. However, if we follow His example, it's not that we suffer or why we suffer; it's *how* we suffer – how we behave, how we act, and how we respond. We don't suffer for the atonement of sin (only Jesus did that), but we may endure suffering as an example to those who do not believe, which in turn, may help them answer the call for their own salvation.

Jesus suffered without sinning – ever![5] In 2:23, Peter was quoting from Isaiah 53:9 when he said that *"He had committed no sin and no deceit was found in His mouth."* There was never a moment in His life where Jesus used a single ruse or smokescreen. He never told a lie, not even a small white lie. He never made a single defense, even when He was being blasted, reviled, and cursed. He never fought back, nor did He ever get trapped in a war of words with others. When He did answer questions, He always answered with God's Word. It is His example Peter is strongly advising that we emulate.

Not once did Jesus even consider retaliation, He simply took everything that was tossed at Him, and then moved along with His purpose and His mission. He didn't threaten anyone, even though He could have. He could have insulted them back, but He never did. He was never concerned with receiving justice on the earth, because He knew that justice would eventually be meted out by the Lord; Jesus placed it all on the Father.

Can you imagine that kind of absolute loyalty and trust in God's sovereignty? It's a struggle to not retaliate in some fashion, either physically or verbally — especially if you are someone who is quick witted or naturally gifted with sarcasm. Jesus could do what He did because of His absolute trust in the Lord, even allowing and accepting the Lord's ultimate judgment. If we follow His example and are able to apply this same degree of restraint, then it makes it easier to forgive others — for anything! If we learn to live by His example, then thoughts of vengeance aren't something that cross our mind, even fleetingly. Paul wrote in Romans 12:19 that revenge belongs to the Lord because every wrong deed is either covered by the blood of Christ or it will be justly repaid by God in the final judgment.

Peter moves on and interposes the idea of healing in 2:24 as further justification for following in the footsteps of Jesus. Jesus never responded in kind to those that tormented Him, leaving their ultimate judgment to God (v. 2:23). Instead, Jesus set His face on His destiny to die on the cross so that we would have a chance to die to sin ourselves and live for righteousness. It is because of Jesus' actions that we can gain not only this gift of righteousness but also healing through His wounds.

There are two competing thoughts and interpretations revolving around the idea of healing.[6] Peter, via the Holy Spirit, is telling us that because of the wounds suffered by Jesus, we are healed. The question is, does this refer to physical healing, or spiritual healing? In this verse, Peter was referring to prophetic scripture from Isaiah 53.

Isaiah 53:4-5: "Surely he took up our pain and bore our suffering, yet we considered him punished by God, stricken by him, and afflicted. But he was pierced for our transgressions, he was crushed for our iniquities; the punishment that brought us peace was on him, and by his wounds we are healed."

Here is what we know.

The word for "stripes" or "wounds" used in 1 Peter 2:24 is *molops*, which describes a full body bruising, a mark on the body by the stripe of the whip. The word *molops* signifies that blood has been drawn and there is significant discoloration and swelling. Peter wasn't sharing this imagery only from revelation or word of mouth: he was there. He was standing nearby when Jesus was being beaten and he heard the rooster crow reminding him of his denial of Christ. So, this event would very likely hold a very deep significance for Peter. It would have marked him for life.

The Greek word for *healed* used in 2:24 is *iaomai* which refers to healing in the sense of a cure, restoring bodily health, or making whole. Another word for healing, that is NOT used in this verse is the Greek word *sozo*, which means "to make well," "to save," "to deliver," "to rescue from death." Most scholars believe that *sozo* is a particular reference to healing in the spiritual sense of salvation as in "to save," "to deliver from," or "to rescue" from an eternal death.

Peter would have written (or dictated) exactly what he heard from the Holy Spirit, what the Lord told him to write. If we believe that the words in scripture are not a mistake, then this means that it was no mistake that Peter used the word *iaomai,* and not *sozo,* in reference to healing.

Therefore, by His stripes [wounds], are we healed "spiritually," or are we healed "physically"? Ultimately, your interpretation is based on what you believe the Holy Spirit is telling you. Is everyone physically healed? No. Similarly, is everyone spiritually healed? While the provision is there, does everyone accept the call for their salvation? No. But it IS God's desire that ALL are healed – physically and spiritually. It is a matter of choice, acceptance, faith, and hope, as well as a complete understanding of the kind of love that God has for each and every one of us.

In verses 2:23-24, Peter is setting us up for the essence of the Gospel message, the example of how Jesus lived His life on earth and why and how He suffered and died so that the goal of His death that we would die to sin and live a life of righteousness be accomplished. Most commentators agree that, by conforming to a life based on the example of Jesus Christ, we rightly witness that He suffered and died for our salvation. If we live by His example, then our own suffering and living our life in a godly manner might influence others to consider their faith in Jesus, just as His death influenced those of us that accepted His call.

Let's go back to Isaiah 53:5 again, which Peter was quoting from, and read once again that "by His wounds you have been healed." Some argue that in 2:24 Peter was only referring to spiritual healing as I alluded to earlier. So, let's go back to the original Hebrew in Isaiah. The Hebrew word for healing in Isaiah 53:5 is *rapha*, which means "to become fresh," "healed," "to mend," "to cure," "repair by a physician." A deeper word study of the word *rapha* will reveal that it makes references to both physical AND spiritual healing.

Therefore, if we compare Peter's word choice in the Greek, with Isaiah's word choice in the Hebrew, then "by His stripes we were healed, " may refer to both physical AND spiritual healing. Perhaps theologians have been getting too analytical and buried in semantics. My own preference is to follow the guidance the Lord places in my heart about this sometimes controversial topic of healing. When sprinkled with the blood of Jesus, I am healed, of everything. And nothing else matters.

Verse 2:25 rounds off Peter's persistence in getting the Gospel message across. We strayed as lost sheep because we were allowing the world and our situations to overtake us. Some of us outright rebelled against God – we denied Him, made fun of Him and those that followed Him. Some of us outright blasphemed. But His promise, His mercy, and His grace allowed us to repent in faith, and then turn around and return to Him and receive salvation. The descriptors of both "Shepherd" and "Guardian" used in this verse are the best definitions of Christ because He is the One that provides us with both guidance and protection, though sometimes, not in the way we expect or prefer.[7]

> *Isaiah 53:6: "We all, like sheep, have gone astray, each of us has turned to our own way; and the Lord has laid on him the iniquity of us all."*

8

Living Godly while Submitting to the Covenant of Marriage and the Church
1 Peter 3:1 - 7 (TPT)

PREMISE

Peter is focused on the principle of wives submitting to their husbands with the understanding that [husbands] who are disobedient to the Word of the Lord will nevertheless take note of the decent and respectful behavior of their wives.[1] This is the same principle shared in the previous two chapters which discussed the idea of submission to authority. Submission is one way that wives serve as a witness to their husbands due to their God-honoring lifestyles.

Wives shouldn't just strive to be beautiful on the outside, but also have beauty in their heart, which is more precious in the sight of God.

Sarah (the wife of Abraham from the Book of Genesis) is mentioned as an example of a wife who was submissive to her husband. Husbands, on the other hand, are told to live with their wives in an understanding way so that their prayers are not hindered.

What makes suffering more difficult for the wife is the wife who becomes a Christian after getting married, while her husband is still an unbeliever. Even though the marriage dynamics will be different, by remaining submissive to her husband, she creates an opportunity to witness to her husband as an ambassador of Christ. While there are other scriptures that refer to the wife submitting to her husband, nowhere else in the Bible do we find the kind of advice that Peter provides about why submission is important outside of obedience to God.[2] Peter is looking to bring harmony to what he hopes will be a Christian household as this strengthens the marriage covenant as they face trials in a godly manner.

Peter concludes this section by strongly admonishing husbands to live in harmony with their wives and to respect and honor their wives as co-heirs of the salvation and grace of Jesus Christ. While wives may be physically weaker than their husbands, both are equal morally, intellectually, and spiritually.

First Peter Chapter 3

[1]And now let me speak to the wives. Be devoted to your own husbands, so that even if some of them do not obey the Word of God, your kind conduct may win them over without you saying a thing. [2] For when they observe your pure, godly life before

God, *it will impact them deeply.* ³⁻⁴ Let your true beauty come from your inner personality, not a focus on the external. For lasting beauty comes from a gentle and peaceful spirit, which is precious in God's sight *and is much more important* than the outward adornment of elaborate hair, jewelry, and fine clothes.

⁵ Holy women of long ago who had set their hopes in God beautified themselves with lives lived in deference to their own husbands' authority. ⁶ For example, our *"mother,"* Sarah, devoted herself to her husband, Abraham, and even called him "master." And you have become her daughters when you do what is right without fear and intimidation.

⁷ Husbands, you in turn must treat your wives with tenderness, viewing them as feminine partners who deserve to be honored, for they are co-heirs with you of the *"divine* grace of life," so that nothing will hinder your prayers.

Living Godly while Submitting to the Covenant of Marriage and the Church

In Chapter 2 of Peter's letter, Peter taught about living as a Christian in a hostile environment, both within the workplace and in society. In Chapter 3 of his letter, he added two more places: the family and the local church. He was insisting that if Christians are to be a witness for the Lord, then they must also be submissive to the social order of things³ (refer back to chapter 6 about submission to authority). This includes our marriages.

Peter's values for the covenant of marriage are in harmony with what Paul wrote in Ephesians 5:22-23:

Ephesians 5:22-23: "Wives, subject yourselves to your own husbands, as to the Lord. For the husband is the head of the wife, as Christ also is the head of the church, He Himself being the Savior of the body."

The Passion Translation advises wives to be "devoted" to their husbands, but other translations use the word "submit" or "subjection." The word "submit," or "devoted" used here in verse 3:1 is the same as the one used in 2:18 (servants being submissive to their masters). This is simply used as a term of recognition for the husband who, biblically speaking, has the role of headship of the household. This is an idea that is becoming less and less popular in the West due to the feminist movement, LGBTQ, and the gender identity debate, but also why the world is in chaos today. Most biblical scholars and theologians interpret this verse (3:1) to be applicable for a Christian woman who is either married to a Christian man or a woman who becomes a Christian after getting married while her husband remains an unbeliever. Nevertheless, if a husband neglects his biblical responsibilities, then the wife will step in.

Let's be clear at the start that women are not inferior to men in any way whatsoever[4], any more than a Christian believer is inferior to an unbeliever (or superior). We will get into more detail about this later; nonetheless, everyone is in a position where they are submitting to someone, or some form of headship (be it a boss, a stockholder, a father or mother, or even business clients in some respect). Wives happen to be in a role that places them in a position of submission to a husband who is the head of the family unit, just as all believers (including men) in a church operate under the headship of Christ.

Within the Old Testament, a Jewish man was absolutely forbidden from marrying a non-Jewish woman (unless she converted); if he did, the couple was evicted from their communities. Similarly, under the New Testament, believers are constrained to marry only other believers as Paul suggested in both 1 Corinthians 7:39 and 2 Corinthians 6:14.[5]

> *1 Corinthians 7:39: "A wife is bound as long as her husband lives; but if her husband dies, she is free to be married to whom she wishes, only in the Lord."*
>
> *2 Corinthians 6:14: "Do not be mismatched with unbelievers; for what do righteousness and lawlessness share together, or what does light have in common with darkness?"*

While 1 Corinthians 7:39 specifically mentions "wife," 2 Corinthians 6:14 implies that the command is also applicable for the husband. Why would the Holy Spirit advise this for the bride but not the groom? For why would the Lord support a Christian man marrying a non-Christian woman, but demand that a Christian woman only marry a Christian man? Either way, Christianity was new in the First Century so it was most likely common that one member of the couple converted to Christianity before the other. In my own personal life, my wife reconnected with Christ after we were married, while I remained an unbeliever for almost 20 years after we married.

That idea that a wife would not be practicing the same religion as her husband at the time Peter wrote this letter was hardly the custom in those times. Greek historian Plutarch (AD 46-127) wrote, "A wife should not acquire her own friends, but should make her husband's friends her own. The gods are the first and most significant friends. For this reason, it is proper for a wife to recognize only those gods whom her husband worships."[6]

Even though Peter is calling on wives to submit, the idea of submission for the wife is one of love, honor, and respect for her husband, which is the way I interpret this verse; however, the wife's devotion is always first and foremost towards her relationship with Christ. We will get into the specific topic of the husband in verse 3:7, but I don't believe the Lord is calling for, nor would He agree with, a Christian husband ruling his house in an authoritarian way, lording over his house like a dictator or tyrant. However, an unbelieving husband likely doesn't care what the Lord has to say on the topic, which makes it more challenging for the Christian wife. Either way Peter is not suggesting that the wife leave her husband, preach to her husband, or demand her rights. It is the gracious and loving submission to her husband that is the strongest form of evangelism she has in her arsenal[7]. This is the way my own wife lived for two decades before I, too, finally accepted His call.

Peter is possibly suggesting in this verse (3:1) that the husband has heard the Word but has yet to believe it and has shrugged it off or denied it. But Peter also implies that the husband's rejection may not be permanent, and that the wife might be able to win over the husband, not by what she says, but by the way she conducts herself; this continues into 3:2.

Peter is advising that a quiet wife is a more appropriate witness[8], and that the focus of her life should be one that is decent and respectful towards her husband – no matter what. This is the same as submission to a boss who is arrogant and prideful as mentioned in the previous chapter. In respect to Christ and the Gospel, the status of the woman has been raised to new freedoms compared with those in the Old Testament Jewish lifestyle (or even pagan lifestyles for that matter), and this could tend to make unbelieving husbands hostile as traditional rules dictated that the wife follow his belief system. Such trends could make the husband feel as if he has lost control.

Peter isn't imposing some draconian, strict "cone of silence" on women, for being "quiet" does not mean "silent." Instead, he is making reference to the Holy Spirit who will advise a woman when to speak and, when she does, to speak with a gentle spirit versus a voice that is antagonistic and degrading. This spirit is more precious to God. Again, Peter is more interested in winning over unbelievers.

It is possible that some women, out of understandable desperation, went beyond Paul's teachings about wifely submission as prescribed in Ephesians 3 and 1 Timothy 2, which gave rise to significant problems in households[9]. Following the Holy Spirit's entreaty, Peter was trying to bring things back under control by suggesting a more conciliatory approach that would more likely win over husbands. Some theologians argue that Peter's advice is very appropriate in today's climate of *egalitarianism*, which suggests that everyone is perfectly equal in worth and moral status (i.e., socialism, communism, income equality, et cetera). The hard truth is that people are not perfectly equal when it comes to man's notions of equality or morality – we are only equal when it comes to God's idea of equality as alluded to earlier.

Nonetheless, when it comes to the idea of the wife remaining silent, we need to keep in mind what Peter will soon write in 3:15 – that all believers need to be ready to give an answer when asked about the hope that lies within them. The idea of silence is simply recommended to maintain peace and appeal within the marriage that would then cause the husband to ask questions.

In verses 3:3-4 Peter is moving on, emphasizing that while desired and appropriate, beauty should not just be displayed on the outside, but also from the inside.[10] He isn't condemning the efforts of the wife to be beautiful for her husband, but that she shouldn't be pre-occupied with it to the neglect of her spiritual character. Also, in some translations, such as the KJV, this verse makes it seem that physical adornment is forbidden, so the NASB, which is also a literal translation, softens and clarifies the verse with the word *"merely"* in italics.

Peter's intent is to prefer inward beauty over external, but not forbidding the external. In 1 Timothy 2:19, the Apostle Paul also encourages modesty in the woman's outward appearance, and instead placing a larger emphasis on the heart. Outward beauty may fade over time from a physical sense (cf. Prov 31:30), but inward beauty never dies unless you allow it.

In verses 3:5-6, Peter appeals to his readers by using the example set by respected women of the Old Testament as a model of modesty, inner beauty, and character to emulate in order to strengthen their determination in how they "dress and make themselves up" – from a godly perspective. If you were to rank who you believe to be the most respected women in the Old Testament, I think that many might place Sarah somewhere near the top. Sarah and Abraham made mistakes (some bad ones actually) and they had flaws just like everyone else, but, as the wife of Abraham, Sarah humbly submitted herself to Abraham because she wanted to; however, as discussed earlier, don't think of the word "submission" as some form of master-slave relationship, or that Abraham was some kind of overlord over Sarah's life – that would be highly inaccurate. Nonetheless, the secular and fleshly will be offended when Peter states that Sarah "obeyed Abraham and called him her lord." Feminists will jump all over this. Yet, Peter uses Sarah as a positive example – as should we all.

Peter is likely making reference to Genesis 18:12, where Sarah said, *"After I have become old, shall I have pleasure, my lord being old also?"* If you look at this verse carefully, Sarah is not speaking to Abraham directly or indirectly. He wasn't even in the area when she said it, so he couldn't hear her.[11] Her use of the word "lord" is not a reference to a master/slave relationship, but a title of respect and honor. Neither within 3:6, nor within other verses, does Peter imply or propose that a Christian wife is supposed to address her husband as lord or master. Nowhere! Sarah was simply expressing a genuine expression of love, admiration, and respect towards her husband.

In 3:6, Peter continues his use of Sarah as an example by stating that women will become a child of Sarah if they do what is right; very similar to the notion that all believers are Abraham's children when, and if, they emulate the faith of Abraham. Paul tells us in Galatians 3:7 that *"those who are of faith...are sons of Abraham."*

Therefore, Peter is implying that it is an honor for a woman to be a spiritual kin of Sarah.[12] Sarah's example of submission to her husband is, according to Peter, something that is right and honorable to God and is part of their spiritual growth. Don't worry, we will discuss the responsibilities of men soon.

If we revisit, for a second, the scenario of some Christian women being married to unbelieving husbands, we can imagine the husband's growing resentment towards her allegiance to God and how he might slander her with verbal abuse, or even threaten her. However, the woman, who may likely be frightened, is not to cave in regarding her faith and must continue to do what is right in a way that honors God, not even knowing where her submission might lead. Moreover, a Christian wife married to an unbelieving husband should carry on in her wifely responsibilities are in the same way that a woman married to a Christian husband does.

After all of this, what does Peter have to say to husbands? It's interesting that Peter squeezes all of his guidance for husbands into one verse (3:7), as compared to six (6) verses for wives. My observation is that this is most likely because women are subjected to more abuse and mistreatment from their husbands than the other way around.

In 3:7, Peter is rounding up his discussion about submission with the topic of husbands, who are also subject to submission, not to wives, but to Christ.[13] While wives are to submit, husbands are also to do what is right, and in this case, it is to live with their wife *"in an understanding way."* This is the key to a good marriage from the standpoint of the husband's obligation and the wife's point of view.

Bottom line is that male and female are different beyond the obvious biology; women will tend to understand their husbands much more than husbands will understand their wives[14]. Peter's words in 3:7 affirm and support what Paul wrote in Ephesians 5:25, *"Husbands, love your wives, just as Christ also loved the church and gave himself up for her."* The husband is to be sensitive to his wife's needs, fears, and feelings; he is also to sacrifice his needs for hers, whether she is a Christian or not.[15]

Peter acknowledges that the woman is weaker from a physical and emotional aspect, but, as implied in 1 Thessalonians 4:4 which says, *"that each of you know how to possess his own vessel in sanctification and honor,"* the woman is equal to the husband intellectually and spiritually.[16] Husbands are to honor their wives as equal heirs of the grace of life, and in doing so, their prayers will be effective. If the husband is not respectful of his wife's needs, his prayers will be hindered.

I believe that Peter is also implying that the marriage covenant between husband and wife depicts the covenant between Christ and the Church.[17] Paul wrote the same in Ephesians 5:22-23:, *"Wives, subject yourselves to your own husbands, as to the Lord. For the husband is the head of the wife, as Christ also is the head of the church, He Himself being the Savior of the body."*

Peter is supporting and augmenting Paul's very specific admonition to elders that they must be good husbands and managers in their home, something that Paul also indicated in 1 Timothy 3:2 and 5:17. Paul points out that elders (husbands) must be above reproach, that they must be temperate, that they must be in self-control, that they must be respectable, that they must be hospitable, and they must be skillful teachers. If the elder doesn't or can't do this at home, then how is he going to take care of the church? How will he represent the church?

While contrary to progressive and Marxist points of view, the idea of the family is a top priority for the Lord, in confirmation of Genesis 2:24, that *"a man shall... be joined to his wife; and they shall become one flesh."* A husband that is abusive, manipulative, tyrannical, disrespectful, or dishonorable to his wife, in public or in private, is one that is being disobedient to God and living a life of sin.

9

When We Suffer for Righteousness Sake, We Do Good, We Don't Do Evil
1 Peter 3:8 - 12 (NIV)

PREMISE

With the word "Finally," Peter is beginning to sum up the message he has been sharing thus far in his letter. After giving us a word about how we should be living our lives in submission to authority and in our marriages, Peter continues by giving us examples of qualities that will allow us to live our lives that bring glory to God. Human relationships are at the core of this section and Peter quotes from Psalm 34:12-16 to help us understand how to deal with people of all kinds. The teaching that Peter shares in this section is consistent with the concepts that Christ Himself taught in Matthew 5:43-44 and Luke 6:27-28.[1]

> *Matthew 5:43-44:* [43] *"You have heard that it was said, 'Love your neighbor and hate your enemy.'* [44] *But I tell you, love your enemies and pray for those who persecute you...'"*

> *Luke 6:27-28:* [27] *"But to you who are listening I say: Love your enemies, do good to those who hate you,* [28] *bless those who curse you, pray for those who mistreat you."*

First Peter Chapter 3 (cont'd)

[8] Finally, all of you, be like-minded, be sympathetic, love one another, be compassionate and humble. [9] Do not repay evil with evil or insult with insult. On the contrary, repay evil with blessing, because to this you were called so that you may inherit a blessing. [10] For,

> "Whoever would love life
>   and see good days
> must keep their tongue from evil
>   and their lips from deceitful speech.
> [11] They must turn from evil and do good;
>   they must seek peace and pursue it.
> [12] For the eyes of the Lord are on the righteous
>   and his ears are attentive to their prayer,
> but the face of the Lord is against those who do evil."

When We Suffer for Righteousness Sake, We Do Good, We Don't Do Evil

In this section of his First Epistle, Peter begins in verse 3:8 by following up with his previous discussion about submission in relationships by providing a list of godly virtues that urge us to be like-minded, sympathetic, loving, compassionate and humble.[2]

- To be like-minded, or to be of one mind, is to be similarly minded, to cooperate with one another in harmony, to think the same, feel the same, and view things the same way, hopefully based on biblical principles and the purpose of being a Christ follower. This provides for similar thinking, similar reasoning, and the ability to come to the same conclusions. Christians are supposed to live an example of peace and unity, not chaos and disharmony.

- When we understand and comfort people, we are being sympathetic to the needs of others.

- By "loving one another," we are bonded together as a family and display a sense of loyalty amongst each other.

- We are compassionate when we are sensitive to the hurts, pains, and misfortunes of others – we hurt when others hurt. The same Greek word *esplanchnisthē* for compassion used in 3:8, is used to regularly describe Jesus throughout the Gospels (Matthew 14:14, Matthew 15:32, Matthew 20:34, Mark 1:41, Mark 6:34, Mark 8:2, Luke 7:13-15). This kind of compassion is experienced as an inward feeling of delight that moves you to do something for someone else.

- When we are willing to listen to others, even when we disagree, we are being humble. A humble person is someone who can think less of themselves and values others above themselves; Biblical humility is grounded in the nature of God. In the KJV and original Greek, it seems that a more fitting word might be "courteous."

A Christian is someone who is strongly inclined to the welfare of those they are committed to.[3] The New Testament strongly enforces the ideals of compassion, sympathy, and brotherly love. As all Christians are children of God, we are a spiritual family and Christ serves as the head (just as the husband serves as the head of the household as discussed in the previous chapter).

The virtues extolled in this verse allow each of us to understand the other and allow for us to see things the same way and have the same goals and purpose. These factors help to prevent the devil from getting into "open doors" and finding access into a marriage or church fellowship, thereby disrupting the unity that is necessary and desired by Christ.[4] But it does take focus and concentration, as our minds tend to wander due to the temptations and stresses of life.

The truth is that there are people around us that challenge each of us to our very core; they turn us off and make it extremely difficult to live the life a Christian is expected to live. Whether an unbeliever or a believer, people will knowingly, or sometimes unknowingly, continue to push our buttons. A common saying used by Christians is, "That person is making it very difficult for me to be a Christian;" however, none of this removes the expectation God has placed on us as His family. When challenged by others, we are to refuse vengeance and fight the desire to retaliate. We should be "that person" that can resist the temptation and turn away anger by providing a gentle answer such as the example set in Proverbs 15:1.[5]

> *Proverbs 15:1 (NIV): "A gentle answer turns away wrath, but a harsh word stirs up anger."*

In 2:21-25, Peter reminded us of Christ's example of not returning evil for evil or insult for insult (i.e., vows of vengeance), but to give a blessing instead, a concept he returns to in 3:9.[6] Let's not forget that he was writing this entire letter to a people who were living under constant persecution and harassment from their detractors. It's easy to give way to vengeance, seeking an eye for an eye when we feel that we have been unfairly treated or judged. The type of blessing a Christian can give to the person trying to instigate us may include finding ways to serve, praying for their salvation, expressing gratitude to them, speaking nothing but good things about them, and a heartfelt desire for their well-being (as opposed to their demise or destruction). I can see some of you shaking your heads or rolling your eyes, but you know this is true. Allow me to be transparent and confess that this is probably one of the most difficult principles for me to follow and live by myself. It's hard to "follow the rules" when others are either ignoring them or are playing by a different set of rules altogether. It is, but this doesn't remove our responsibility to follow God's Word. We stick to His will for us and should not follow "that" path back into man's rules.

The idea is not that you have to be perfect at it, but to be diligent and honest in your efforts to work towards it. The Lord knows your heart. So the way we, as believers, respond to conflict, disappointment, and offenses is extremely important. The goal is to be empowered to walk in peace, experience unity that does not break, and to remain spiritually strong as God intends.

In 3:8, Peter provides us with the five virtues we should live by and then, in 3:9, he warns us against personal vengeance. He is reminding us that, no matter what is happening around us, we are to be like-minded, sympathetic, compassionate, humble, and have brotherly love. This definitely challenges what is at the core of most men – our desire to be protectors and providers, our desire to roar like a lion. But we need to remind ourselves *Who* we are living for. What is the larger witness? So we should remember to remain calm and relaxed when we are being slandered or abused, not to act out and beat the crap out of someone or gossip junk about them in your circles of trust or on social media (even if passively aggressive)?

This verse (3:9) carries with it the reminder that God Himself gave us an undeserved blessing instead of judgment[7] – forgiving someone for a wrongdoing is free; it doesn't cost you a thing other than making a choice, whereas judging others comes at a cost (our thought life, our heart life, et cetera). What we sow, we will reap. If we get caught up in a war of tit for tat, it becomes a vicious cycle, an exhausting back and forth loop, of sowing and reaping bitterness, anger, and resentment.

Our testimony, our godly witness, should be one that blesses others because we have been called to inherit a blessing. If you were set to inherit a 100 million $$'s but under the strict condition that YOU must always be nice to people "no matter what," that you must openly and transparently forgive and exhort those that are attacking you, that you should bless others when they gossip about you – could you and would you? Oh yeah, and you would need to have a camera and microphone on you 24 hours a day. If you should ever violate this condition, you would lose it all. How do you think you would behave? Could you do it? Or would a day or two of personal relish, which would only be temporary, be worth giving it all up? This same analogy comes up again in a later chapter.

What do you think characterizes those who are of God? Let's not confuse this with protecting yourself or others against physical harm or death – I do believe we have a right to protect ourselves, but there is a process we operate through when operating in the condition of self-defense (peace is ALWAYS our first course of action; walking away is ALWAYS our second). But, what if someone slaps you, or someone starts calling you all sorts of names, or insults your wife or kids? "These are fighting words, right?" Perhaps this is why Peter makes references to Psalm 34:12-16.

> Psalm 34:12-16 (NIV):
> 12 Whoever of you loves life
> and desires to see many good days,
> 13 keep your tongue from evil
> and your lips from telling lies.
> 14 Turn from evil and do good;
> seek peace and pursue it.

> *[15] The eyes of the LORD are on the righteous,*
> *and his ears are attentive to their cry;*
> *[16] but the face of the LORD is against those who do evil,*
> *to blot out their name from the earth.*

During the period that Jesus was walking the earth sharing His ministry, He always led by example what is exemplified in this Psalm, but He never fully experienced the blessings that are promised – not until He ascended to Heaven.[8] It was His purpose on earth to suffer for sin, not to experience the blessings; however, you and I aren't living on this earth to suffer for sin, but we are called to suffer with Him while simultaneously experiencing the blessings that He did not. Therefore, we really ought to consider Peter's advice as a matter of our witness and testimony, more than any benefits we receive on earth.

When that anger rises and the tension increases in our bodies, our mind swarms and our body shakes, but we must refuse to take offense, we must refuse to be bitter and express all of the other negative emotions that come well up. As Christ followers, we really ought to be looking to Jesus to help us discern the situation properly and then react the way Jesus did. One single, right response can diffuse and de-escalate a volatile situation. This allows us to be the blessing we are meant to be, which we get into more in the next verse.

In 3:10, Peter is quoting from Psalm 34:12-13. Here's the deal, men: we will NEVER be able to control what others say or how they say it, but we CAN control what we say and how we say it. The flesh wants to do what the flesh wants to do, but since we are spiritual people, we ought to do what the spirit wants to do, not our flesh. Yep, it's hard; nevertheless, this is the life we signed up for. This is why many either refuse His call, or, they give up after a period of time.

The fact is that the result of being a "blessing" to others, as also pointed out in verse 3:9, is that we tend to love life more and experience more good days than bad. We can experience a rich and joyful life, even while surrounded by hostility and junk that we believe is stupid and ignorant. The only requirements for a full life are that we live humbly with a loving attitude towards everyone (as outlined in verse 3:8), partake in pure and honest speech (as outlined in verse 3:10), disdain sin and pursue peace (as we will find in verse 3:11), and have right motives that please the Lord (as we will see in verse 3:12).

In 3:11, Peter is quoting from Psalm 34:14 and is reminding us that the ability to love life and experience a blessing will come to those who can keep their tongue from evil and do good[9] (in other words, stop talking smack and live peacefully). Our goal in life is to turn away from things that are sinful and evil, but it's also much more than that – we need to actually pursue things that bring peace. Is this hard to do today? Yep, absolutely. But maybe, just maybe, it's men like us that can actually bring this about, if we agree to unite together, rise up, and continuously operate this way. Why not? What's the downside? Pride? Ego? The idea that we are following rules that others won't, or don't? The path to God's blessing is obedience to God in our daily life, not just when we feel like it. And yes, we may sometimes suffer as a result; something that we have already been told by Peter to expect. In contrast, disobedience will always lead to God's discipline, and it is God's discipline that we need to fear more than the dude that is making you angry.

In 3:12, Peter is quoting from Psalm 34:15-16. One of the guarantees we have in life is that the eyes of the Lord are always on us, the righteous, and He does hear our prayers (I didn't say He answers all of them, at least not specifically, directly, or in a way that we imagine).

The *"eyes of the Lord are on the righteous"* so that He can observe and care for them. None of us will ever know how many times we have been pulled from the jaws of death until the day arrives that we are standing in front of Him.[10] How many vehicle accidents did He prevent? How many items did we suddenly see that prevented us from tripping and falling downstairs? How many times did we suddenly catch ourselves before slipping on ice and breaking a bone or two? How many times were we engulfed in violence and yet, miraculously, walked away unscathed? Okay, that one may be limited to a smaller number but you get the point. Sometimes, the Lord answers prayers in ways that we don't see or perceive as an answer. Sometimes, the Lord saves us when we didn't even know we were in danger. Sometimes, the Lord may not answer a prayer because the prayer is not in accordance with His will, or, He knows that answering that prayer may destroy us or lead us astray.

"His ears are attentive to their prayer" so that He can meet our various needs and cares. However, the truth is that sometimes this doesn't mean that He will keep, or prevent, believers from suffering; but it does mean that He will provide His grace in ways that *"strengthen and establish"*[11] believers who are in the middle of

suffering and in great times of need. This is something that Peter digs deeper into in Chapter 5 of First Peter, where he discusses the principle of purifying our faith.

Another truth is that sometimes we believers get caught up in things that cause us harm: War, Storms, Criminal activity. But I firmly believe that those of us that earnestly seek to walk in righteousness and live the way God wants us to, are spared much more often and blessed much more frequently than others.[12] Lest we forget that He also saves us from ourselves, let us appreciate those moments when He brings to light something we are about to do that is "not cool." He often sends us warnings when we are completely unaware. Praise God!!

10

Undeserved Suffering While Following Christ and Living Godly
1 Peter 3:13 - 22 (NET)

PREMISE

*It may seem odd and even irrational, but in this section of his letter Peter is nudging us, perhaps not subtly, to the ideal that Christ followers are blessed even when they are suffering, **IF** – big if – they are suffering for the sake of righteousness.[1] This is similar to how he addressed the topic of suffering in verses 2:21-25. The assertion is that through the sanctification process, Christ is sanctified in our hearts to such a degree that non-believers will ask us about our faith and we, in turn, are prepared to give an answer.*

Bottom line is that Christ died to bring people like you and me to the Father² so that we can help others like us. Towards the end of this section, Peter touches on the act of baptism as it relates to how Noah and his family were saved from the flood because of the Ark – which symbolizes death followed by resurrection.

Peter is advising us to be prepared to share why we have hope, to maintain a good conscience, and to remain aware of Christ's suffering and purpose.³ We are to ALWAYS be ready! Verses 3:19-21 are touted by some as one of the most difficult passages to interpret in the Bible,⁴ yet the revelation remains that Christ suffered and died for sin in order to bring His people to God.

In the letter Peter points to Christ's example of innocent suffering at the hands of this world's citizens. The culminating is that Jesus' innocent suffering, death, resurrection, and exaltation, are the very foundation for the salvation and vindication of believers.

First Peter Chapter 3 (cont'd)

¹³ For who is going to harm you if you are devoted to what is good? ¹⁴ But in fact, if you happen to suffer for doing what is right, you are blessed. ***But do not be terrified of them or be shaken***. ¹⁵ But set Christ apart as Lord in your hearts and always be ready to give an answer to anyone who asks about the hope you possess. ¹⁶ Yet do it with courtesy and respect, keeping a good conscience, so that those who slander your good conduct in Christ may be put to shame when they accuse you. ¹⁷ For it is better to suffer for doing good, if God wills it, than for doing evil.

¹⁸ Because Christ also suffered once for sins,
the just for the unjust,
to bring you to God,
by being put to death in the flesh
but by being made alive in the spirit.
¹⁹ In it he went and preached to the spirits in prison,

²⁰ after they were disobedient long ago when God patiently waited in the days of Noah as an ark was being constructed. In the ark a few, that is eight souls, were delivered through water. ²¹ And this prefigured baptism, which now saves you—not the washing off of physical dirt but the pledge of a good conscience to God—through the resurrection of Jesus Christ, ²² who went into heaven and is at the right hand of God with angels and authorities and powers subject to him.

Undeserved Suffering While Following Christ and Living Godly Before the World for Righteousness Sake

Verse 3:13 immediately comes off as almost being contradictory.⁵ Peter states that if we are zealous for good, then who can harm us? However, back in verse 2:20 he told us that if we suffer for doing good, then it is commendable to God. So if we are with God for good, can people harm us or not? Will we suffer or not? He then continues with what appears to be another contradiction into the next verse (3:14). But wait, it will clear up, so stay with me.

The truth is that while it may seem unusual for anyone to hurt those who are benefiting society, who are kind and caring, it does happen. In some translations Peter begins verse 3:14 with *"Even if,"* or *"If you happen"* as shown from the NET used in this chapter. This indicates that Peter was writing to people who were already suffering for their faith; therefore suffering is not improbable – it is to be expected. Seems contradictory from 3:13, doesn't it? Suffering is a symptom of a fallen world.

After telling us in 2:20 that if we suffer for doing good, then it is commendable to God, and later telling us in 3:13 that if we are zealous for good, then who can harm us, Peter continues in 3:14 by advising us that even IF we should suffer for the sake of righteousness, then we are blessed.[6] Okay, kinda close to semantics, but it's not. Being blessed implies privilege and honor.

> *James 1:2: "My brothers and sisters, consider it nothing but joy when you fall into all sorts of trials..."*

In verses 2:10 and 3:14, Peter uses the Greek word *pascho* for "to suffer." This word means to experience a sensation or impression that is usually painful. However, this is not necessarily a reference to physical things. Suffering can come in many forms such as emotional torment, societal and cultural torment, slander, et cetera. Then in verse 3:13, Peter uses the Greek word *kakoo* for "to harm." This means to injure or to exasperate, a reference to being highly irritated or frustrated.

In Romans 8:31, Paul asks us *"If God is for us, who is against us?"* Well, those opposed to God are against us and they will endeavor to make life as difficult for us as they can (at times). When Peter is making reference to suffering in 2:20 and 3:14, he is telling us that Christians will definitely suffer; it will happen. But, in 3:13, he is also saying that we won't come to harm as a result of this suffering if we remain focused on what is good in the eyes of God. Believers may receive verbal backlash, ridicule, and more, but it can only harm, irritate and frustrate us if we allow it to and/or if we decide to take God out of the equation. We need to recognize that simply being for God does not mean, or imply, that the suffering will necessarily stop.

Peter concludes 3:13 with a basic reference to Isaiah 8:12-13, inspiring believers not to be intimidated by those who are trying to irritate and frustrate them[7] (i.e., to harm them), but to face them with the fear of God. Intimidation in this verse is the Greek word *phobos*, which means "to be put in fear;" Peter's advice in this regard is to continue with your life being sanctified by Christ, which he digs into more in verse 3:15.

> Isaiah 8:12-13: [12] "Do not say, 'Conspiracy,' every time these people say the word. Don't be afraid of what scares them; don't be terrified. [13] You must recognize the authority of the Lord of Heaven's Armies. He is the one you must respect; He is the one you must fear."

Peter is admonishing believers in 3:14 to not give into the fear mongering of those trying to intimidate them – almost implying that they fear you, which is why they are trying to irritate and frustrate you in the first place. Those that choose not to believe in Christ can't make sense of why believers have a fear of God, nor can they comprehend why their fear of God is stronger than their fear of man.[8] Some argue that this is because a Christian's faith grants them a degree of confidence that to some defies rational comprehension.

Since the heart is where Jesus resides, this is also where He prefers to be worshipped. To sanctify, in the modern sense, means to make holy as far as God is concerned[9] – a process that begins with our initial justification, followed by ongoing sanctification, and ending with eventual glorification. However, most believe that Peter is making reference to the Old Testament use of the word, which means "to set apart," such as "setting apart" vessels that are specifically for God's use.

Sanctifying Jesus as Lord implies that we are making Him the center of our lives[10], an approach that keeps us prepared for anything that comes against us that may require some form of defense or testimony to others about our belief. This also serves as a provision for courage for the future, which either helps us get through our present challenges, or gets us through to the day that we eventually pass from the earth. Think about what this meant for the First Century Church when persecution was rampant in their communities, society, or court systems.

The word for "defense" used in 3:15, (or "an answer" as used in the NET for the purposes of this chapter) is the Greek word *apologia*, which is where we derive the idea of apologetics.[11] Peter uses the word in an informal sense, insisting that believers must understand what they believe and why they are Christian in the first place. You should then be able to articulate your beliefs in a way that is humble, thoughtful, reasonable, and biblically sound. Believers should always be able to provide a rationale for why they believe what they do, but in a way that is charming and righteous. "Charming and righteous" can be difficult for some that are naturally brash or sarcastic, but with the Holy Spirit, even they can do it.

Peter concludes this thought in 3:16 with a concern that believers remain gentle (or courteous) and respectful, as the way we conduct ourselves can impact our witness to others[12] (an argument that Peter makes multiple times throughout this letter). We need to guard our hearts against becoming arrogant and prideful, or even from getting unnecessarily preachy. Some believe that the only arguments that matter in these cases are the stories about our experiences and why we have hope. Whatever your belief happens to be in this area, one thing is certain: we need to watch our behavior and maintain a good conscience as non-believers are constantly looking for excuses to point fingers at us to declare "Aha! Gotcha!"

Sanctifying Christ as the Lord of our hearts gives us an attitude of having moral and ethical standards as outlined throughout scripture, which serves to prepare us when a defense and/or a testimony is necessary.[13] This also serves to protect us from slander and unsubstantiated gossip – meaning that others should automatically know when lies are lies without a doubt in their minds. We should not allow slander to impact our conscious and deflect us from the path the Lord has set.

On the other hand, a bad conscience accuses you and makes you experience guilt, shame, doubt, fear, anxiety, or despair. A free life, one lived under the command and authority of the Lord, produces a "good conscience" which causes false accusers to feel the "shame" of their own conscience.[14] It is part of the cycle of sowing and reaping. A free life under God reaps a good conscience, whereas false accusations will reap a bad conscience. It may not happen immediately to the false accuser, but it will happen eventually, even if we have to wait until we die. Wait! What?

One of the unfortunate truths is that, sometimes Christ followers are not always vindicated, and they continue to suffer from the slander and gossip – no matter how hard they try to overcome it. The comfort we still have, in this case, is that the Lord Himself will ultimately judge the attacker (false accuser), which is one reason why we can maintain courage during those difficult times. As difficult as it may be, you may never experience personal satisfaction on earth – let's be honest about that. This is likely why Peter was concerned that believers maintain a spirit of gentleness and respect as outlined in verse 3:15 earlier.

Verse 3:17 is an example of a New Testament "shift and lift" from the Old Testament. In the Old Testament, people suffered when they did wrong, while they were blessed when they did good.[15] But in the New Testament, the principle is that you should expect to suffer even for doing good. A primary reason for this is, in the Old Testament, faith was pretty much limited to the borders of Israel and portions of the surrounding nations (such as Arabia). However, in the New Testament, the Christian faith has a global reach. The Church's mission is to share and witness the truth throughout the world, not just within the borders of one's country. The act of witnessing to the entire world of the 21st Century places Christ followers in more resistant locations today, and in more hostile territories than during the first century, which by itself increases the danger to Christians in many ways.

In verse 3:18, Peter reminds us that Christ suffered and died as the righteous One in place of the unrighteous so that we, the unrighteous, would be brought closer to God. This verse covers what some refer to as the "Doctrine of the Cross" or "Theology of the Cross."[16] The first points to the idea that "Christ also suffered for sins once for all," as also pointed out in Hebrews 7:27.

> *Hebrews 7:27: "He has no need to do every day what those priests do, to offer sacrifices first for their own sins and then for the sins of the people, since* **he did this in offering himself once for all***." [emphasis mine]*

The NASB version of Hebrews 7:27 more accurately proclaims that Christ suffered for our sins for "all time," implying that His sacrifice has no time limit: it is infinite. Under the Old Covenant, the Jews would sacrifice animals on a regular basis (such as Passover) and the high priest would offer sacrifice for the nation on the Day of Atonement once a year. The covering was perishable and had to be repeated year after year. However such sacrifice is no longer required as the sacrifice of Jesus covered ALL sins, for the WHOLE world, for ALL time (He is Imperishable). This thought flows into the "Doctrine of grace" as it makes working for our salvation no longer a necessary component of our faith.[17]

Several translations of this verse offer thoughts about the cross with the words "the just for the unjust." Christ sacrificed Himself for the unjust while He Himself was the just, as a form of justice for our sin, not His.[18] This concept is explained more deeply in Romans 3:21-30, specifically, verses 23-26.

> *Romans 3:23-26: "[23] for all have sinned and fall short of the glory of God. [24] But they are justified freely by his grace through the redemption that is in Christ Jesus. [25] God publicly displayed him at his death as the*

mercy seat accessible through faith. This was to demonstrate his righteousness, because God in his forbearance had passed over the sins previously committed. [26] This was also to demonstrate his righteousness in the present time, so that he would be just and the justifier of the one who lives because of Jesus' faithfulness."

Believers were unrighteous in their behavior "Before Christ," but, through their faith in the Messiah, the Lord provided righteous judgment through the event of their justification and, as a result, believers are now counted righteous in their lives "After Christ." This doesn't give us permission to continue in sin; that would be willful disobedience and considered unrighteous, for Jesus did not die to give us permission to simply have a better day or continue behaving the same way with the same attitudes. No, the righteous live their lives with a pure heart, striving to be holy (but never fully holy, which we will dabble into in a later chapter).

Peter continues his analogy to the "Doctrine of the Cross" with his words *"So that He might bring us to God,"* which pertains to the believer's reconciliation (reconnection) with the Father. Reconciliation is something that happens by the will of God, by His forgiveness of our sins, and by the obedience of our faith to follow Him. The concept of reconciliation is discussed in more detail by Paul in his second letter to Corinth, specifically 2 Corinthians 5:17-21.

Reconciliation is by the will of God.

[17] "So then, if anyone is in Christ, he is a new creation; what is old has passed away—look, what is new has come! [18] And all these things are from God who reconciled

us to himself through Christ, and who has given us the ministry of reconciliation"
(2 Corinthians 5:17-18).

Reconciliation is by the act of forgiveness.

"In other words, in Christ God was reconciling the world to himself, not counting people's trespasses against them, and he has given us the message of reconciliation" (2 Corinthians 5:19).

Reconciliation happens by the obedience of faith.

"Therefore we are ambassadors for Christ, as though God were making his plea through us. We plead with you on Christ's behalf, "Be reconciled to God!"
(2 Corinthians 5:20)

How can God forgive sins and be just?

"God made the one who did not know sin to be sin for us, so that in him we would become the righteousness of God" (2 Corinthians 5:21).

The bottom line is that the believer is now at peace with God and is no longer alienated from Him – we have been reconciled (i.e., reconnected).

The final idea that Peter shares regarding the Doctrine of the Cross is the fact that Jesus became human so that it would be possible for Him to die; it was not possible for Him to die in His divinity.[19] He was *"put to death in the flesh"* by this evil world (the physical realm) so that He could be *"made alive in the spirit"* through the connection of the Holy Spirit in the heavenly realm. Some translations capitalize the word Spirit to emphasize the dominant role of the Holy Spirit in this passage.

In verses 3:19-22, we begin to enter into an area of scripture that many consider to be one of the most difficult passages to interpret.[20] I agree it is a difficult passage, but I would personally consider passages from the Book of Revelation to be more challenging due to the degree of symbolism, analogy, and metaphor. In either case, this portion of the letter studies the suffering of Christ on the cross more deeply as it relates the believer's proclamation of faith discussed in 3:15 that believers who suffer need to be ready to make a defense and testify about their faith.

In verse 3:19, Peter makes mention of "spirits in prison." What is the deal with "spirits in prison"? There is quite a bit of debate about this, and I found differing opinions in the commentary of the CSB (Holman), ESV (Crossway) and NKJV (MacArthur).[21] I believe we need to continue into verse 3:20 as we look for help with the answer.

These "spirits" could be all those that were disobedient and died in the flood during the times of Noah. In 3:18, Peter mentions that Christ was "in the Spirit" which continues through to the end of verse 3:20. It is suggested by theologians and scholars that the reference to Christ being "in the Spirit" in verses 3:18-20, is also a declaration that Christ was also present "in Spirit" during the flood from Genesis and that He preached through Noah, further implying that it was Jesus' proclamation to those Noah was attempting to reach.

As these unbelievers in the time of Noah heard the "good news," but chose not to obey, they are now suffering God's judgment "in prison." In 2 Peter 2:5, Peter refers to Noah as a "herald of righteousness" which means that Noah was preaching. In 1 Peter

1:11, Peter mentions the Spirit of Christ operating through the Old Testament prophets, which supports the argument that the Spirit of Christ could also have been operating through Noah. Finally, Noah was being persecuted as part of a minority of believers, as were Christians during the time that Peter was writing this letter. As God saved Noah, God is expected to save current believers as well. It is noteworthy that Peter also mentions Noah and the ark in 3:20.

Another idea considered by theologians (the Holman CSB, for example) is that the "spirits in prison" are "some of the fallen angels (or evil angels) who were currently in confinement." It says "some" of the fallen angels because not all demons are bound to this abyss (prison, as seen in Luke 8:31). However, the problem with this interpretation comes in the form of a question? Why would Jesus not have proclaimed victory to ALL of the fallen angels, not just a grouping of them? He could have proclaimed victory to those not in prison as well, but He didn't.

The third idea considered is that the "spirits in prison" are the "sons of God" referenced in Genesis 6:1-4, who many believe were angels who cohabitated with the "daughters of men." But such sexual unions seem unlikely as Jesus compares the future resurrection of believers to angels in Matthew 22:30, who have no gender and don't marry.

Based on scripture as a whole, and my belief system, I believe that the *"spirits in prison"* is a reference to those who were disobedient in the times of Noah and were obviously dead at the time of Jesus' sacrifice on the cross. If we read verses 3:18-20 carefully, it seems to me that Jesus visited these "spirits in prison" and proclaimed victory to them while they were in "prison," after His resurrection but before he ascended to Heaven. The Greek word for "prison" is *phulake*, which means a place where someone is watched, guarded, or kept in custody. Poetically speaking, Peter was referring to hell, or the abyss, where demons and the souls of wicked men are committed and condemned.

Therefore, "the spirits in prison" are those who were disobedient to God as He patiently operated through Noah to preach to them while he built the Ark in preparation for the flood, a time period that most theologians agree lasted for at least a hundred years. The reference in 3:20 to "the patience of God...in the days of Noah," as reflected in the time that Peter wrote his letter, is a great example of how God operates to warn sinners over a long stretch of time. He doesn't try to get our attention for only a few minutes, or just one time, or three times; He tries to get our attention throughout our lifetime.

The Ark that Noah built saved eight people **_through_** the water (as opposed to being saved **_by_** the water). This is analogous to the hard truth that, even today, not everyone will be saved, which further alludes to the type of suffering Noah endured as he preached to his generation who were unyielding in their unbelief.[22] As believers strive to reach the unsaved, there are only two possible results – the disapproval of those who hear the message, or, the salvation of those who praise it.

In verse 3:21, we begin to see a connection between the flood in the days of Noah and water baptism by Christ followers today (as well as New Testament examples). If you don't truly understand the concept of baptism, then this explanation may bless you. Believers are saved ***through*** the water of judgment; hence, baptism portrays ***salvation through judgment***. Let's dig into this more deeply.

Eight people were saved ***through*** the water and now, *"baptism now saves you... **through** the resurrection of Jesus Christ."* The eight people were not saved by the water, but through it. The water served as final judgment for the disobedient during the time of the flood, but it does not save the obedient today any more than it saved the eight people in the Ark – it was the Ark (representing Christ) that saved because it remained afloat during the flood.[23] To be saved, you must go ***through*** the "flood"...not stand off to the side in wonder.

What could have been a disaster for those eight people became a means of salvation, because of the Ark. As the water from the flood served as judgment for the disobedient, Jesus' death serves as God's judgment on sin. As the Ark served as the salvation of the eight people onboard, Jesus' sacrifice serves as salvation for believers to this day.

The NASB uses the word "corresponding" at the beginning of verse 3:21, whereas the NET quoted in this chapter uses the word "prefigured." In either case, the original Greek word is *antitupon*, which is where we get the term antitype, which means corresponding to, counterpart, or representative. The flood corresponds to or represents Christian baptism. Or if you prefer, Christian baptism represents the flood.[24]

Just as with the flood, the water in baptism does not save anyone, but, just as the ark saved the eight people through the water, baptism is symbolic of the death of Jesus on the cross, which is the act that saves people to this day. This is why Peter reminds is that baptism saves us, not because it removes dirt from our bodies but acts as an appeal to God through the resurrection of Jesus Christ.[25] The act of baptism itself DOES NOT SAVE; it is because of our faith of His action on the cross, which is symbolized by the water, that saves.

Your water baptism represents your inward faith, as evidenced by one's "appeal to God" as mentioned in 3:20 for the forgiveness of sins (so that I may have a good conscience). Belief that sins are forgiven through the death of Christ and the believer's act of faith through baptism is the "answer of a good conscience." This is why many link baptism with the outward sign of one's faith and symbolic of the person's salvation. That is the reason the early church strived to perform baptism as soon as possible after believers chose to believe in the gospel, as indicated in Acts 2:38. Today, some folks wait for a year or longer, or they get baptized when Pastors determine it is time to place baptism ceremonies on the calendar – what a shame!

> *Acts 2:38: "Peter said to them, 'Repent, and each one of you be baptized in the name of Jesus Christ for the forgiveness of your sins, and you will receive the gift of the Holy Spirit.'"*

Regardless of denomination, all Christians generally believe that water baptism is an outward sign of the inward reality of regeneration which is the result of the work of the Holy Spirit, and something that is only received by grace through faith. I would prefer that Pastors conduct baptisms just like they do weddings – when a person wants to get baptized, they schedule time with their pastor who should accommodate that request as soon as possible.

The bottom-line up-front message of this entire section is that Jesus has triumphed over His enemies and is now ascended to Heaven to His place of eminence, honor, majesty, authority, and power. As mentioned in the closing of 3:22, Jesus now sits at the right hand of God in heaven with all things being subjected to Him. It is in from this position that all believers will ultimately reign with Christ.

11

Leave the Past Behind and Remain Spirited in Your Love 1 Peter 4:1 - 6 (NCV)

PREMISE

The opening words of 4:1-2 set the theme for this section. Christ suffered while He walked the earth "in the flesh,"[1] meaning He was physically here in the same type of earthly body that you and I have. Something that Christ did while in His physical body that we are to strive to follow by example is to not give in to the temptations that our bodies want, but to give in to the will of God that our spirit needs.

In our lives "before Christ," we lived just like the Gentiles are described in scripture, giving in to our personal desires and physical passions. In our lives "before Christ" we hung out with people and did things with people that we now know, "after Christ," to be wrong. The people

155

from our past life are going to be shocked, and possibly even alarmed or threatened by this new attitude – are you now going to pressure them to convert as well? They may even be hurt by the fact that you now refuse to do those things with them.

The hope that Peter has, in this letter, is that, living by the example of Jesus, believers will show to others that this life is not dead and boring, but alive and exhilarating.

First Peter Chapter 4

[1] Since Christ suffered while he was in his body, strengthen yourselves with the same way of thinking Christ had. The person who has suffered in the body is finished with sin. [2] Strengthen yourselves so that you will live here on earth doing what God wants, not the evil things people want. [3] In the past you wasted too much time doing what nonbelievers enjoy. You were guilty of sexual sins, evil desires, drunkenness, wild and drunken parties, and hateful idol worship. [4] Nonbelievers think it is strange that you do not do the many wild and wasteful things they do, so they insult you. [5] But they will have to explain this to God, who is ready to judge the living and the dead. [6] For this reason the Good News was preached to those who are now dead. Even though they were judged like all people, the Good News was preached to them so they could live in the spirit as God lives.

Leave the past behind and remain spirited in your love

Beginning with 4:1, Peter is advising Christ followers to live by the example of Christ who *"suffered in His body,"* and to be prepared to live for the same purpose that Christ lived. Paul also stated

something similar in Romans 6:10 when he reminded us that Christ

"died to sin once for **ALL"** (emphasis added).

> Romans 6:10 (NIV): "Yes, when Christ died, he died to
> defeat the power of sin one time—enough for all time. He
> now has a new life, and his new life is with God."

The word *"body" (flesh)* used by Peter is neither a spiritual

metaphor nor an analogy, Peter is reminding us that Christ literally

suffered on the cross in a physical body just like you and I have – it

was 100% flesh. It is not an accident that Peter uses this word for

flesh in 4:1 and again in 4:2. This repetition reminds us that Christ

suffered a physical death and that, as believers, we will cease to sin

just like Jesus,[2] after we die – obvious for human beings, right? But

how does this apply to those of us still living?

A full review of Romans 6:1-11 shows that God considers

believers to be dead *with* Christ.[3] When we die with Christ – a

metaphor for giving up our old life for a new life following Jesus – we

identify with His death, with His burial, and with His resurrection.

This "ceasing" to sin (or *"finished with sin"* as the NCV translates it)

that Peter mentions in 4:1 does not mean that believers won't

continue to sin, but that believers are to arm themselves with the

attitude that they are done with sin, period. Believers are to be

determined, meaning focused and disciplined, to live a life with Christ

that is unmistakably different (meaning the difference is obvious)

than the life they were living "before Christ"...a thought that Peter

continues in 4:2.

In 4:2, Peter refers to *"no longer of human lusts"* (the NCV writes *"not the evil things people want"*), meaning that by whatever patterns we lived in our lives "before Christ" that kept us from Him, these patterns should no longer be allowed. The expectation is that we now live "for the will of God," meaning that we do what God wants us to do, how He wants us to do it, and how He wants us to say it.

By holding on to this attitude of the spirit instead of giving in to our "lusts" and "temptations," we know, with an infinite degree of confidence, that we will be in a much better place if, or when, we face persecution. I know what you are thinking, and I agree: this is difficult if we see our earthly hopes, values, and desires being torn apart or dashed. But we need to place in the forefront of our minds that the very day we accepted Jesus Christ we abandoned the lusts of men and are ceasing from sin. Not ceased, ceasing.

If there is something that you want to say, or do, in response to something that someone did or something that someone said to you, you will know if that action or verbal response is consistent with the will of God or not. You will also know that if you go against it and do it anyway, then you are operating in sin. Peter adds to this "spiritual logic" in 4:3.

Think about the amount of time you spent in your life "before Christ," now let's put that into perspective as it relates to what Peter is telling us in 4:3, *"you wasted too much time doing what nonbelievers enjoy,"* basically, "you've already wasted enough time, why would you continue wasting more of it?"[4] Peter follows his "waste of time message" with a list of bad behaviors that, if we are honest, most of us either indulged in or are presently indulging in: lust, drunkenness, carousing (i.e., raising hell), drinking parties, and hateful idol worship.

It is this list of behaviors Peter put together that we are to put behind us; he labels them as the desires "of the Gentiles" (or nonbelievers). Now, with caution, I am going to share that I like beer and I like a snip of bourbon now and then, but I never allow myself to get drunk – I typically drink water at the same time. So, I don't believe that a beer or two, or a glass of bourbon is sin – not in my case anyway. But it does cross the line if: 1) you are an alcoholic or used to be, or, 2) if you get drunk or even buzzed. Alcohol is not medication nor a form of sedation – be extremely careful with this.

The item in the list that some may have a hard time interpreting is "wanton idolatries" - some translations say, "abominable idolatries" or "hateful idol worship" in the case of the NCV as used in this chapter of this book. Wanton, or abominable, is the Greek word *athemitos*, which means "unlawful" or "lawless" as opposed to righteous – therefore "wanton" means sexually unrestrained or promiscuous. So, it would seem that Peter was referring specifically to sexuality in the sense of this verse. "Idolatries" comes from the Greek word *eidololatria*, which also means "image worship" or "covetousness."

It is possible that Peter is warning us against coveting sexual activity that is unlawful and unrestrained such as adultery, forced or unwanted sex, orgies or group sex, sexual activity that is a form of temple worship, having numerous partners, or possibly, even specific sexual acts.[5] Jewish traditions, both modern and in the biblical era, already held to a list of vices that were condemned, implying that Jews were already not party to these sorts of things. This is why Peter makes the reference of this list to Gentile desires and behavior. This is also why I agree with the idea that Peter was writing this letter to primarily Gentile converts as opposed to Jewish converts as discussed in the opening chapters of this book.

Peter recognized that Gentiles may struggle with their new Christianity perhaps a little more than Jewish converts and is suggesting that our past lives, and the past relationships that we may still be holding onto, may put pressure on us to slide back into our past sinful behavior. If you don't fall under that pressure, as you shouldn't, this may cause some resentment from those you used to, or still do, hang out with, something that Peter moves on to in 4:4.

When I was a teenager, I was pretty deep into the drug scene of the 1980's era in the Los Angeles/Long Beach area, something I entered into around the 8th grade. I smoked pot and eventually got into crystal meth; my primary motivation was a desire to bond with my friends and feel like I was part of something. A few years later, probably around my junior year of high school, my friends started doing acid, but I refused as I already felt bad enough about using crystal meth. As you might imagine, as teenage boys do, they made fun of me, they teased me, they mocked me, and they even cussed me out and called me all sorts of names; yet I steadfastly refused to the peer pressure to do acid. Eventually, their constant attacks on me angered and frustrated me enough to "walk away" and, after four years of friendship, I left them and never hung out with them again. I literally cut it off 100%.

I fractured that bond with my "friends" but it came at a cost as I needed to reinvent myself at a very young age. I did, and I grew in the process (partially). Now let's be clear; I wasn't a Christian then and I still continued smoking pot up until a few months before joining the military, but the story I share is an example of that all too familiar "social pressure" or "peer pressure" working on us. If unbelievers will do that to other unbelievers – I did not use God or faith as my excuse not to do acid – imagine how unbelievers might react to believers when they use their faith, no matter how it is articulated.

To bookend my story, a few years after walking away (I was in the military at this time), one of my "friends" disappeared for over a week before being found in the trunk of an abandoned car alongside a highway road in Los Angeles. He had been murdered. To this day, I am still amazed that some of my other friends were shocked and surprised by this – I wasn't surprised at all because it was blatantly obvious to me based on the path we had been walking together. Based on this bookend to my short story, I obviously do not regret walking away that day in the summer of 1986 – that friend could have been me. In contrast, believers in Christ should likewise not be surprised when things happen as unbelievers continue to walk their chosen paths; yet unbelievers will question, "How did this happen?" The same "shock and awe" should not surprise us as believers when we or others stray and God disciplines us.

Paul tells us in Romans 2:14-15 that even unbelievers instinctively know what God's Law requires and they often follow their instincts.[6] However, it is more often that they suppress their instincts, they ignore what they know to be right and true, and then they violate it. However, when believers follow the Truth, it somehow pricks at the conscience of unbelievers and might make them dislike you – not you, specifically, but the faith that you are following. Your faith represents a reminder to them that they are doing wrong – and they know it, but they do it anyway. Your faith convicts their conscience and makes them uncomfortable and shameful. They don't like that feeling and they will likely manifest a form of denial and self-justification. But, as Peter tells us in 4:5, *"they will have to explain this to God"* one day about their conduct and behavior.

The reference to *"living"* in 4:5 is a literal reference to those that will be alive at the time of judgment, and those who are *"dead"* being those who died before the day of judgment.[7] Bottom line is that we will all be judged eventually. However, it is noteworthy that Peter doesn't mention those who haven't been born yet; most biblical scholars believe this is because it is likely that Peter thought Jesus would return in his lifetime. However, I think scholars might be over thinking it or over spiritualizing it. Those that had yet to be born in Peter's day would either die before Christ's return or they would be alive at the time of His return. They will either be living, or they will be dead. Either way, this verse applies to those of us reading Peter's letter today, just as much as it did to the people he was writing to at that time and those who will be reading it a hundred years from now.

The possibility of everyone's salvation (thus their justification), including those yet to be born, is outlined in verse 4:6 where we find another one of those difficult phrases to interpret: *"to those who are dead."* The word for *"dead"* in 4:6 is the same word used in 4:5, the Greek word *nekros*, which literally means "physical death."

A lot has been made about the phrase of *"those who are dead,"* with some commentators suggesting that the gospel message was literally preached to the dead, but this makes no sense. The message was preached to those who are "now" dead, implying that they heard the message when they were alive.[8] Even though the gospel message we know today was not taught prior to Jesus, a semblance of the gospel message was taught in the times of the Old Testament.

In the New Testament, the *Gospel* in preaching about the good news, ironically and literally, talks about the death and resurrection of Jesus Christ and how believers are to respond in repentance, forgiveness, and faith.[9] In the Old Testament, the *Gospel* message was about a prescription of sacrifice for atonement, and that ultimate sacrifice was made plain by Isaiah's prophecy in Isaiah Chapter 53 with the detailed revelation of the coming Messiah. The message of that time did not include anything in reference to discipling the nations, but it was communicated through the testimony of Israel and its people. When Jesus came to earth and died on the cross, the gospel message taught in the Old Testament had been made complete. Before Jesus, it was a "come and see" message, but after Jesus, it became a mission to "go and tell."

12

An Attitude of Urgency and Ethics for the End Times
1 Peter 4:7 - 11 (VOICE)

PREMISE

Believers live knowing that the end is coming. And because of this, we should be living committed in love while also serving as good stewards of the "spiritual" gift(s) the Lord has given us by His grace. Believers are to speak as if God were speaking and should serve so that in all things Christ might be glorified.[1] Easy, right?

First Peter Chapter 4 (cont'd)

[7] We are coming to the end of all things, so be serious and keep your wits about you in order to pray *more forcefully.* [8] Most of all, love each other steadily and unselfishly, because love makes up for many faults. [9] Show hospitality to each other without

complaint. [10] Use whatever gift you've received for *the good of* one another so that you can show yourselves to be good stewards of God's grace in all its varieties. [11] If you're called upon to talk, speak as though God put the words in your mouth; if you're called upon to serve others, serve as though you had the strength of God behind you. In these ways, God may be glorified in all you do through Jesus the Anointed, to whom belongs glory and power, now and forever. Amen.

An Attitude of Urgency and Ethics for the End Times

In 4:7, Peter definitively declares that the end is near, that it is imminent. I usually chuckle to myself when I hear Christians say this today – of course each day is closer to the end. It is mathematically, logically, and rationally the most single accurate fact in the world today. Christ can return at any moment and begin His reign. But, until that day, persecution is guaranteed to come and go, like waves crashing on the shore. The good news is that Peter tells us how we ought to be in the present (today), which is sound (i.e., grounded) and sober in spirit and prayer. The Voice, which I used in this chapter, says it this way, *"be serious and keep your wits about you to pray more forcefully."* If we don't do this, the routine of life will numb us and cause us to be caught off guard when things don't go the way we expect or desire.

Beyond telling us to remain serious and keep our wits (sober and grounded), Peter zooms in on two more areas that provide us with the necessity of remaining expectant and determined. In 4:8, he reminds us that, above anything, we are to remain committed in our love for one another; in this case, he is referring specifically to other believers. This type of supporting love is what allows us to remain encouraged and involved both before, and during, challenging times when things seem to be contrary to us.[2]

The Bible refers to love as a verb – an act, not an adjective or an emotion. Because it is an action word, the Bible can command it as a decision that believers can make[3]; it's a choice to do something (or not). Either way, it is this kind of love for our Christian brothers and sisters that builds the community and strengthens the body. Be honest, have you ever wanted to throat punch someone or scream at them in a way that is "shock and awe"? If you did that, what do you think would happen when you, or that person, are experiencing trouble at some point in the future? Lack of love erodes trust; lack of trust erodes confidence; lack of confidence erodes fellowship. Love is the best attitude adjustment tool.

Peter was quoting from Proverbs 10:12 when he wrote, "*love makes up for many faults.*"

> *Proverbs 10:12 (VOICE): "Hatred fuels dissension, but love calms all rebellions."*

As Peter has alluded to numerous times so far in this letter, the goal is to win over unbelievers, and the kind of love he is describing here gives us what we need to prepare ourselves to forgive those that cause us problems or serve up strife.[4] We must be prepared to love because we are likely not ready for that kind of love, the kind that Christ expects, in the beginning of our walk with Christ. Some are, many are not.

In 4:9, Peter tells us that, in addition to remaining committed in our love for all of our brothers and sisters, we also need to be hospitable – and not complain about it. But check this out: "hospitable" in the Greek is *philoxenos*, which means being kind and loving strangers. This means that we also need to be hospitable to those who don't agree with our faith – and not complain about it. In today's political climate (2021), are you in a position to love and care for someone who is politically opposed to you? Perhaps. Could you be just as hospitable and loving if they wanted to share and push their political views on to you?

Part of the process of preparing us for the ups and downs of persecution is a willingness to help all strangers, which is an extension of the command to love our brothers and sisters. At the time Peter was writing this letter, it would have been difficult for travelers to find a place to stay, but a Christian home was the answer (and solution). Additionally, as the First Century church was starting to expand, there would have been numerous disciples and apostles that would need a place to stay while serving and traveling as missionaries.[5]

Every believer who has been born of the spirit and declares that Jesus is Lord has received at least one spiritual gift from God as Peter alluded to in 4:10; gifts that were not earned but gracefully provided by Him. This gift was also given to those who are insecure or suffer from low esteem. The NASB (which is a literal translation) includes the word *special* in italics to emphasize that the gifts are not just standard gifts but special and unique as given by God.[6] These would include your abilities, your skills, and your talents. These gifts aren't supposed to be hoarded, but faithfully used to meet the needs of others, as stewards of God's grace.

These gifts are not to be confused with talents that are developed by your own ability or your time spent years in training; these gifts are a reference to gifts supernaturally and divinely imparted by the spirit of God.[7] Some people may refer to a person with these gifts as a prodigy, or a savant – with abilities that people pick up suddenly with little to no training. Gifts like this, that people see, are typically in the area of music, the arts, or even in mathematics, but we rarely hear about the savant with special gifts in gardening, or in leadership, or in counseling, or painting, and so on. You can also include those who have a special gift of exhortation or lifting up people when they are downcast or upset. The Apostle Paul also discusses the gifts of the Spirit in 1 Corinthians 12:7-11 and Romans 12:6-8.[8]

Peter doesn't discuss or provide a list as Paul did. He may have believed that his readers were already aware of what spiritual gifts are, and he exhorts us to use them. There are some who wait on their gifts to manifest like some kind of supernatural event before they are willing to step out and use their gifts, but folks like this usually end up very frustrated.

> *1 Corinthians 12:7-11: "[7] Each believer has received a gift that manifests the Spirit's power and presence. That gift is given for the good of the whole community. [8] The Spirit gives one person a word of wisdom, but to the next person the same Spirit gives a word of knowledge. [9] Another will receive the gift of faith by the same Spirit, and still another gifts of healing—all from the one*

Spirit. [10] One person is enabled by the Spirit to perform miracles, another to prophesy, while another is enabled to distinguish those prophetic spirits. The next one speaks in various kinds of unknown languages, while another is able to interpret those languages. [11] One Spirit works all these things in each of them individually as He sees fit."

Romans 12:6-8: "[6] Since our gifts vary depending on the grace poured out on each of us, it is important that we exercise the gifts we have been given. If prophecy is your gift, then speak as a prophet according to your proportion of faith. [7] If service is your gift, then serve well. If teaching is your gift, then teach well. [8] If you have been given a voice of encouragement, then use it often. If giving is your gift, then be generous. If leading, then be eager to get started. If sharing God's mercy, then be cheerful in sharing it."

Other translations, such as the KJV, include the word "minister" as a gift. To minister means to be a committed and professional servant who is highly motivated to serve at the highest degree possible. The gifts are given to us to minister to others as well as reveal God to man.

Some of us are waiting on what we believe will be the perfect time to explore and use our gifts, but God is waiting on us to take ownership of them and use them now. History shows that for those who have made dramatic moves in their calling, they started that process based on a simple decision to just move. When God gives us gifts, He expects us to be stewards of them just as we would treat something that we treasure and highly value.[9] When we use these gifts, we must remember to give God all of the glory (I am guilty of forgetting this way too often) for these gifts are not for our benefit or self-promotion. Living the life of a Christ follower means living by grace through the Holy Spirit; it is this grace that allows the gifts to operate in our lives.

It's time for you to recognize what God has placed inside of you so that you can begin using the gifts as God expects you to; it's up to you to start releasing them now for the benefit of those around you. He may prompt you on occasion, if you are listening and can hear His prompt. Or, He may simply be waiting on you to exercise what He has clearly placed inside of you. He's already done His part; now it's time for you to do yours.

Concluding on the topics of gifts, love, and hospitality, Peter warns believers in 4:11 to speak words that are actual words of God (in other words, speak what you believe God is speaking, or if you prefer, speak what you believe God wants you to speak). However, when you are speaking, one thing is very clear: make sure that you speak in a way that honors and glorifies God.[10]

Paul lists out speaking gifts in 1 Corinthians 12:8-10: words of wisdom, words of knowledge, words of prophecy, tongues, and interpretation of tongues. Some commentators also include teaching and exhortation as speaking gifts as outlined by Paul in Romans 12:6-8, which makes sense since these require actual speaking in a way that blesses others.

Finally, if we refer back to Peter's commentary about hospitality towards strangers earlier in this section, in 4:11 he is highlighting possible opportunities for evangelism and, perhaps, preaching. In this case, it is paramount that whoever is speaking, "speak as though God put the words in your mouth." Grace should be part of the impartation.

13

Suffering Through Fiery Ordeals for the Glory of God
1 Peter 4:12 - 19 (NASB)

PREMISE

Christ was persecuted while He physically walked the earth, so it shouldn't be a surprise to Christ followers today when they experience "fiery ordeals."[1] Why should it be a surprise? Jesus' message is the same today as it was 2000 years ago. If we share in the suffering that Christ endured, it should be expected – what's more, Peter says that we should rejoice in it. Furthermore, if Christians suffer at the hands of "evildoers" or those that tease and mock the Gospel of Christ, then they shouldn't be ashamed when they suffer – if they are suffering for the sake of Christ. If Christ followers truly believe that they will eventually be judged, how much more do you think people who disobey the Gospel will be judged?

The ESV commentary states that God uses Christian suffering as a way to purify the Church, which is why Christians need to give themselves over to God without crying and complaining. All the same this is another one of those scriptural examples of something that is easy to listen to or read but a tad difficult to live out and do – this is our flesh fighting our spirit. We will break this down in this chapter.

Peter explains that four attitudes are necessary in order to be triumphant in persecution: 1) expect it (v.12), 2) rejoice in it (v. 13, 14), 3) evaluate the cause (v. 15-18), and 4) entrust it to God (v.19).[2]

Verses 4:12-19 deal with the reality of the world in which we live, which becomes more apparent by the opening words in 4:12, "don't be surprised when fiery ordeals come." Junk doesn't typically happen by accident; usually someone did or said something that caused the "fiery ordeal" to occur.

The truth is that sometimes we experience issues and challenges in life that suck and/or are very painful – that is the reality of living in this world (it's a fallen world, right?). The truth, as far as believers are concerned and fully aware of, is that the very essence of humanity has been affected by the fall of humanity itself. Believers and unbelievers alike can be very friendly and hospitable one time, while they can be cruel and downright mean the other.

For those of us that live in the USA, we are blessed to have laws that allow and sanction religious freedom (as of March 2021 anyway); however, this does not mean that we shouldn't expect not to suffer from discrimination from time to time. In some instances, we bring it on ourselves, but discrimination still happens anyway. The choice of Christians to live a lifestyle that is Gospel based is considered very radical to unbelievers and might even serve to aggravate them as previously noted in 4:4 and discussed in an earlier chapter. The very idea that we would live and preach a life that salvation only happens through Christ is considered by unbelievers to be pompous, disdainful and discriminating.[3] In fact, it irritates, frustrates, and angers many of them, which is why they lash out, another reason that believers should not be surprised when crap happens to them.

First Peter Chapter 4 (cont'd)

[12] *Beloved, do not be surprised at the fiery ordeal among you, which comes upon you for your testing, as though something strange were happening to you;* [13] *but to the degree that you share the sufferings of Christ, keep on rejoicing, so that at the revelation of His glory you may also rejoice and be overjoyed.* [14] *If you are insulted for the name of Christ, you are blessed, because the Spirit of glory, and of God, rests upon you.* [15] *Make sure that none of you suffers as a murderer, or thief, or evildoer, or a troublesome meddler;* [16] *but if anyone suffers as a Christian, he is not to be ashamed, but is to glorify God in this name.* [17] *For it is time for judgment to begin with the household of God; and if it begins with us first, what will be the outcome for those who do not obey the gospel of God?* [18] *AND IF IT IS WITH DIFFICULTY THAT THE RIGHTEOUS IS SAVED, WHAT WILL BECOME OF THE GODLESS MAN AND THE SINNER?* [19] *Therefore,*

those also who suffer according to the will of God are to entrust their souls to a faithful Creator in doing what is right.

Suffering Through Fiery Ordeals for the Glory of God

The *"fiery ordeal"* used in 4:12 comes from the Greek word *purosis*, which refers to a trial or the smelting that occurs in a furnace. From the context of this verse, Peter is advising that Christians shouldn't be surprised when trials happen. Scripture, and the vast majority of commentary, points out that "suffering is the norm." Scripture and commentary regularly use the word "suffering," but I find this word to be difficult to truly comprehend for some of us today in contrast to the degree of suffering in the first century, or, for Christians today in places like the Middle East or many African nations. I don't believe Western Nations, Americans in particular, truly understand "suffering" as used in the scriptural context.

As stated in the premise of this section, junk in our lives doesn't typically happen by accident. Usually, someone did or said something that triggered the "fiery ordeal." The bottom line is that whenever people are involved, stuff is just going to happen. Christ won't let you down, but people will.

One commentator stated that the use of "fiery ordeal" is similar to the word *holocaust*, such as the Jewish Holocaust.[4] A holocaust is typically referred to as a calamity of biblical proportions, so I suppose this interpretation is permissible. But I don't believe Peter was speaking figuratively of an ordeal of this magnitude at the time of writing. I do believe he was speaking about suffering in the form of discrimination, ridicule, slander, and even being made to feel like the dregs of society.

James wrote in James 1:2-4 that Christians ought to consider it a time of joy when experiencing trials because it tests our faith and produces endurance; this is part of the perfecting and sanctification process. The difference between James and Peter is that James was speaking in more general terms, whereas Peter was referring specifically to suffering. "Fiery ordeals" are not strange; they are normal, and that is the reality. However, what one person may consider a "fiery ordeal" might seem like the proverbial "cake walk" to others.

In 4:13, Peter says, *"to the degree"* that Christians *"share the sufferings of Christ,"* that is the extent to which we are to keep rejoicing. In simpler terms, while we are partnered with Christ in His suffering, Peter is saying that we will never experience the same level of suffering He did, but a degree of it – and we should keep rejoicing anyway. Easier said than done! But why would Peter encourage this? So that others around us can see and experience the glory of Jesus through us. The way I see it, when we live in joy, even when things in our life might be horrible, unbelievers will have one of two thoughts: 1) we are simply weird, or 2) there must be something to this "Jesus" thing. The one lost sheep is worth it.

The secondary effect of rejoicing while suffering is that it reduces the physical impact on our bodies – even if only a little. There are many benefits to living a positive lifestyle, even when surrounded by negativity and chaos. Of course, the degree of rejoicing we live by will also be measured and tempered based on the knowledge we will be rewarded with in eternity. How does your faith stand on the prospect of your future reward, no matter what you are going through right now?

If you were told that you have a $100 million inheritance in your future but it came with guidelines that would challenge you and your belief system, do you think there is a threshold of suffering, or "suckiness" that you would reach where that $100 million fortune is no longer worth it? Or would you endure whatever was necessary, no matter what? A Christian who is persecuted for righteousness in this life should have overflowing joy because of his future reward. Just as with the $100 million future inheritance, it is this awareness of the future that gives us joy today, no matter what is happening around us.

Christ was insulted when He was walking the earth, so it shouldn't be a shock when Christ followers are also insulted as they are following Him the way scripture prescribes. Peter tells us in 4:14 that we should consider it an honor as it is evidence of the Spirit of God and the glory upon you. How does that make you feel? For some, they can smile at suffering and shrug it off like nothing; for others, they carry it around as a burden and get frustrated and irritated, wanting to retaliate in some way.

This was one of the biggest fears I had when I was first born again – the mocking, the teasing, the dread of being humiliated whether to my face or behind my back. Why did I have this fear? Because that's exactly what I did to Christians and how I behaved for a LONG time! So I stayed in the closet with the exception of those closest to me.

For some, our natural tendency might be to focus on our own faults and shortcomings when rejected or ridiculed for our faith in "the name of Christ;" but this is exactly what the devil wants you to do. As Peter reminds us in 4:14, the truth is that *"you are blessed"* because you have been chosen by God and are part of His elect (refer to how Peter opened this letter in 1:1-2 as discussed in Chapter 3). And because you are part of His elect, *"the Spirit of glory, and of God, rests upon you."* This is why Peter was exhorting us to rejoice back in 4:13.

So, while our natural inclination might be to dwell on our faults (shame, guilt, blame, etc.), it is God's natural inclination to lift us up during those moments of defeat.[5] The natural result will be that others will visually see the blessing we experience while suffering and they may want the same thing. This is when the Holy Spirit begins to break down their natural barriers[6] (as well as the ones they've been trained, taught, and educated to have), and allow them to see God's glory. Paul writes in 2 Corinthians 2:15-16, *"for we are a fragrance of Christ to God among those who are being saved and among those who are perishing."*

When insecurities pop up, some may question how we can know if our sense of rejection is our fault or if it is due to "the name of Christ" within us? One answer given by Peter is to examine, or take inventory, of your "current" life. (DO NOT reflect on your past life.) When we suffer as believers, for any reason, it is God's presence that specifically rests on us and lifts us up with strength and endurance – sometimes beyond what we originally thought was physically and emotionally possible.

If you are a murderer, a thief, an evildoer, or a meddling troublemaker, then perhaps your rejection is justified – this is why Peter is advising us, in 4:15, not to be, to do, or participate in any of that "stuff." We can find out if we are party to any of it by examining ourselves, which is the only way that we can *"make sure that none of you suffers"* from any of the sins Peter lists.

Peter is striving to deal with the type of things that will "lead" to persecution, from revolutionary disruptive kind of things to being a jackass in the work environment. A Christian living in, or working in, a non-Christian culture is to do his work faithfully and live virtuously in a way that honors Christ. This usually draws out questions from skeptics, or even from Christians, that don't understand how this principle applies to such historic events as war or combat. How about America's fight for Independence from England? What about a person who serves as a whistleblower in the workplace or in government?

It's therefore crucial that you consistently examine yourself:
1) What has God called YOU to?
2) What has God equipped YOU with?
3) Is there peace in YOUR heart "and" YOUR spirit?
4) What is God telling YOU right now?

If it all checks out, go for it with the knowledge that God will judge you righteously. If there is even one RED X, then perhaps you ought to pray on it more.

I sure would hope that these sins are not part of the Christian lifestyle, though "troublesome meddler" might be subjective. For example, Christians inserting themselves into the topic of abortion is considered meddling by some; on the other hand, many feel that they are called and ordained to be activists in this area by God. However, sometimes, Christians simply intrude, or inject themselves, into things that belong to someone else to deal with. What has God called YOU to and what has He equipped YOU with? Emotional passion may not necessarily be from God; it could be your own flesh. God will only equip you with everything you need if He has called you to it. Else, it is our godly duty to stay out of it.

As long as we check our hearts and sense the Lord's approval, then we can presume our "meddling" is not a sinful act in whatever you feel led to intervene in. I suspect that many of you might agree that there are Christians inappropriately meddling in affairs that are none of their business – like busybodies.[7] Or they come across as foolish because they are not yet equipped to do it and show themselves to be inarticulate or insufficiently informed on the subject matter in question.

It shouldn't take much effort to look at ourselves and the way we are living. If, after examining yourself, you find that your conscience is clear and God is pleased, yet you are still suffering for the simple fact of being a Christian, then Peter reminds you in 4:16 that you have nothing to be ashamed about. We are to continue living our lives as Christ followers while giving glory to God.

The reality is that everyone will ultimately be judged, both those in the Church and those who are not. *"The household of God"* refers to the temple, and God's people are His temple as referenced back in 2:4-10 (see the discussion in Chapter 5), which outlined how God's people are like living stones built up as a spiritual house.

In 4:17, Peter advises us that the Church, meaning believers, will be judged first, before those that disobeyed the gospel. Peter brings this out by asking a question that contrasts God's judgment of believers with His judgment of unbelievers; it also appears he is referring to the judgment that will occur after Jesus returns. That the Church would be judged by God first, makes sense logically, rationally, and more importantly, spiritually (the glorification process perhaps?).

Verse 4:17 is often used to reinforce the priority for believers to serve as a good witness to the rest of the world. It is also used as part of the character development process[8] for Christians as was previously outlined in 4:12, and further reinforced in James 1:2-4 regarding testing during the "fiery ordeal."

Interestingly, Peter doesn't say what the outcome of this judgment might be for believers or unbelievers, but, if taken in association with other scriptures of the New Testament in totality, we can safely assert that the outcome for unbelievers will be condemnation[9], while believers will be rewarded. He clarifies this in 4:18.

In 4:18, Peter is quoting from Proverbs 11:31, indicating in the first half of the verse that the righteous will be saved, but asking a question in the second half – what is going to happen to the godless and the sinner? But it goes deeper than that as Peter points out that it is with "difficulty" that even the righteous will be saved, indicating that some of the righteous barely make it: it is that close. If then the justified sinner is saved with "difficulty" while suffering pain and loss, what do you think will be the end for the ungodly?

In Proverbs 11:31, Solomon emphasizes that the righteous will be rewarded, but the wicked and the sinner will also be rewarded "much more." The rewards we receive will be based on the judgment we receive as Peter outlined in 4:17. The Message paraphrase of Proverbs 11:31 writes that if the good barely make it, what's up for those that were bad? As the New Testament testifies to over and over again, there is no salvation apart from grace through faith and acceptance of Jesus Christ.

Peter concludes this section of his letter in 4:19 by further exhorting those *"who suffer according to the will of God"* to place their complete and total trust in God to be fair and do what He promised – that He will take care of us for doing what was right while obeying Him.[10] When you give your life to God, you are pretty much giving him back what He originally created. As your Creator, He knows what you need more than you do. No doubt, this is a difficult proposition from a worldly perspective, capable of earning you eyerolls and laughter from those that don't believe.

But, if we don't place our trust in Him, how else are we going to manage and get through the fiery ordeals and all the stuff that happens to us as we live and conduct ourselves according to His Word? The ridicule, the slander, the mocking, the name calling, and more? The greater our confidence, faith, and trust in Him, the more that stuff will roll off of us while we still live joyfully, serving as a witness to those that are doing the mocking. We MUST place all of our dependence on God. Oh, but that pride! The struggle is real but it doesn't mean we should stop pressing forward in our faith.

14

Leading the Flock of God Willingly and with an Attitude of Responsibility
1 Peter 5:1 - 5 (KJV)

PREMISE

Peter begins to shift focus as he starts to close out his letter. Peter identifies himself as an Elder among Elders to those he is writing this letter to. It is likely that he included himself as an Elder to emphasize his credibility, give support, and highlight his position as a personal witness of Christ's suffering – he was there.[1] "Elders" is a biblical and scriptural reference to those who hold the pastoral office of the Church; it is used interchangeably in scripture with the words "shepherd," "pastor," and even "overseer"(Titus 1:5-7).

Peter is urging his readers to be honorable and responsible servants to the people they have oversight of: it is a huge responsibility. The biblical and scriptural terminology refers to this as "shepherding the flock," the flock being the children of God and Jesus being the Chief Shepherd. Shepherds of the New Testament Church have been charged with nurturing, leading, and protecting God's people without dominating or manipulating them.[2]

Jesus will eventually crown those who served honorably and faithfully with unfading glory, despite their personal suffering; this reward includes those who are young in the faith who are honor bound to respect their Elders. All congregants are to operate in humility, for God opposes the proud while giving grace to the humble.

This section closes on the idea of humbly submitting to church leadership, outlining both the costs and opportunities that come with this role.

First Peter Chapter 5

[1] The Elders which are among you I exhort, who am also an Elder, and a witness of the sufferings of Christ, and also a partaker of the glory that shall be revealed:

[2] Feed the flock of God which is among you, taking the oversight thereof, not by constraint, but willingly; not for filthy lucre, but of a ready mind;

[3] Neither as being lords over God's heritage, but being examples to the flock.

⁴ And when the chief Shepherd shall appear, ye shall receive a crown of glory that fadeth not away.

⁵ Likewise, ye younger, submit yourselves unto the Elder. Yea, all of you be subject one to another, and be clothed with humility: for God resisteth the proud, and giveth grace to the humble.

Leading the Flock of God Willingly and with an Attitude of Responsibility

I used the KJV translation for this Chapter where verse 5:1 jumps straight into addressing the Elders of the Church. In other translations, such as the NASB, TPT, and ESV, verse 5:1 begins with *"Therefore,"* or *"So,"* or *"Now,"* meaning "for that reason," and pointing to the previous portion of scripture; it implies that what follows will describe what the previous passages mean to the reader and why they are important and critical. I don't know why some translations added the extra emphasis at the beginning of 5:1, but what Peter speaks to in this area of his letter is, nonetheless, something that we really ought to pay attention to. If necessary, I would encourage you to go back and read the previous 5 or 6 verses of the last chapter before moving forward. In this section, Peter is going to focus specifically on the leaders of the church, while simultaneously developing what he has already shared with the Church as a whole. And once again, he is being real and raw about suffering and persecution, but now he is going to focus on what church leaders are supposed to do during these "fiery ordeals."

When the Church or its members suffer through trials and/or persecution, this is when its most reputable leadership is crucial. The "Elder" is a person who is filling the role of Shepherd, a person who is spiritually mature and emotionally intelligent. The word "Elder" is translated from the Greek *presbuteros*, a word borrowed from the Jewish synagogue as it draws a picture of experience, wisdom, and authority.[3] It is one of four words used in the New Testament to designate leadership: "pastor," "shepherd," "overseer," "bishop," and, of course, "Elder." But "Elder" is used more frequently within the New Testament, which may surprise novice readers of scripture as a heavier emphasis from the pulpit is generally placed on "pastor."

That Peter was writing in the plural to a group of Elders indicates that there is, traditionally, more than one Elder per church body who helps to oversee and take care of God's children[4] (i.e., the flock). In both First and Second Peter, Peter often reminded his readers that suffering, in some fashion, typically precedes glory. Elders have a responsibility to aid the entire congregation, which in some cases in the First Century Church, was large and spread over large areas (urban and rural), requiring more than one Elder. Keep in mind that there were no church buildings, per se in the First Century Church and most congregations met in larger public spaces, or, in their homes.

As the First Century Church was being planted in various villages, cities, and regions, it was typically always accomplished through the efforts of the Apostles (of which Peter is obviously one). An apostle was normally attached to a local church, sometimes referred to as the "Home Church," and he was regarded as an Elder of that local church.[5] But he also served the churches within his jurisdiction both in ministry as well as the primary source of revelation and teaching to the local church Elders; thus, he would be an overall authority figure over several churches. By pointing out that he was also an Elder in addition to his role as an Apostle, he is by default, also a partaker of the same glory that regular church members enjoy. Peter was working to motivate his readers through his own humility and exhortation.

Peter is including the Elders in the same grouping that he views himself, implying that he is not superior simply because of his seniority in the Church. Nonetheless, Peter did not shy away from noting that he was a personal eyewitness of Christ's suffering[6] (see Acts 1:21-22). Peter was motivating his readers through their anticipation of the future, that one day they would receive a reward from the hand of Jesus Christ Himself for the services they were fulfilling in His Name. This interpretation is also confirmed in verse 5:4, which makes further reference to rewards at the judgment seat of Christ. Knowing that Peter had personally witnessed Christ's suffering and His transfiguration (meaning His resurrection and dramatic transformation in appearance on the mountain as witnessed by His inner circle, Peter, James and John), and personally participated in the Lord's glory, gives Peter added credibility with his readers.

A side note in reference to Elders, as opposed to the often-used term "deacon." The distinction between Elder and deacon is a matter of debate among Christians because of two different arrangements of deacons and Elders.[7] In some cases, there were multiple Elders in each house church supplemented by deacons, with a division of responsibilities between them, arranged at local levels, or within specific house church bodies. Typically, local church culture will dictate the differences between the deacon and an Elder along biblical guidelines.

After Peter motivates his readers in 5:1, he begins to exhort them in 5:2. The primary role of the modern-day Elder is to provide oversight, which partly consists of the command to "feed the flock;" which means to teach, and *every* Elder should be able to teach.[8] Elders are also supposed to protect the flock from ideas and influences that would cause them to deviate from the faith. In any case, the flock belongs to God, not to the Elders, and not to the pastor. If any church leader imposes some form of authoritarian ownership over responsibility, this is a sign that pride has reared its ugly head.

Again, Elders should never feel "compelled" to serve but serve "willingly," as instructed by God; they should not serve simply because they were asked by another leader in the church. If you are asked to serve as an Elder in your church, you might feel flattered, and you might feel an adrenaline rush (caused by emotion), but you really *need* to take it to God. Are you called to serve in this capacity *and* has God told you to accept that invitation? An Elder, as a shepherd, has responsibility for the care and protection of the souls of the members of the congregation. This is *serious* business.

Most theologians believe that in 5:2 Peter was advising Elders not to be lazy, warning them that laziness is one of the first dangers that they would be confronted with.[9] The idea is that the demands of the task, along with the divine calling of serving as an Elder, would prevent Elders from being lazy and indifferent. They should be motivated to serve, and to only serve for the benefit of God and the flock. Why? Because false teachers are always prowling around and motivated by the second danger facing Elders – money, or *"filthy lucre"*

Scripture indicates that churches should pay their shepherds, but true shepherds, which includes pastors and Elders, should not use their power and influence to rob people of their wealth, either through coercion or manipulation (yet, even the Church is not immune from illicit activity as we, unfortunately, know has happened, is happening, and will happen – even Jesus' discipleship team fell victim to this with Judas). A desire for undeserved money should never be the reason that a pastor or Elder serves.[10] This is one of the major complaints of the Church today (primarily in denominational churches and/or churches that preach the prosperity message).

Though he did not, I wish Peter had included "pride," because I believe that we, the Church (capital C), often place people in the position of Elder for the wrong reasons (friendship, family member, tenure at the church). Some are consumed with themselves rather than others, which is not living as a servant. Serving as an Elder has become a way of elevating certain people in modern society while sidelining those who are serving honestly and with the right heart. Men in particular are seeing this, at the cost of a decline in male membership (as of early 2021) as evidence of this. Right-minded members are tired of what they perceive, some legitimately and some not – the fakeness, the wokeness, and the hypocrisy of some that are serving in positions of leadership for "political" reasons.

However, in contrast, some people are asked to serve as an Elder when they have never considered themselves qualified or, even if they felt qualified, never jostled for power. I believe it is people like this that can be the GREAT teachers and influencers we read about – those that don't seek their own advancement. In this case, it is the Holy Spirit guiding the process, not men. Only if the position of Elder is regarded as servant leadership – which is the biblical principle – can motives be pure.[11]

Another way Peter describes the wrong motivation for the office of Elder is found in 5:3 – the desire to exercise authority simply for the sake of personal power. "To lord over" means to dominate someone over particular situations and events. So, the temptations for Elders include laziness, finances, and now, demagoguery, which is seeking support by appealing to the prejudices of people rather than being rational. Peter's implication in this verse is that Elders should not lead by manipulation or intimidation but through true spiritual leadership, and living and serving by example.

"Lording over" also involves the manipulation of people rather than leading people for their highest good. In short, lording is a worldly model of leadership that Jesus said was forbidden to His disciples.[12] It's possible that Peter was recalling Jesus' own words from Matthew 25:25-28 (which he heard himself because he was there), and he may even have learned this lesson himself through personal experience or observation at other churches.

*"But Jesus called them unto him, and said, Ye know that
the princes of the Gentiles exercise dominion over them,
and they that are great exercise authority upon them. But
it shall not be so among you: but whosoever will be great
among you, let him be your minister; And whosoever will
be chief among you, let him be your servant: Even as the
Son of man came not to be ministered unto, but to
minister, and to give his life a ransom for many"*
(Matthew 20:25-28).

The word "pastor," both as a noun and a verb, is derived from the process of shepherding God's flock and Peter reminds Elders of the responsibilities they have been entrusted with:

1) To shepherd (to pastor) the church gladly and willingly in accordance with God's will, and not out of compulsion,

2) To do the work (to pastor) eagerly and not out of greed or for shameful gain, and

3) To serve (to pastor) as examples to the congregation, and not use their place of leadership as a means of being domineering.

All you have to do is pay attention to the news today, particularly over the last 10-20 years, to understand the impact of Peter holding these responsibilities as important. When violated, they not only hurt the Elder/Pastor who is caught abusing his position, but they also create a problem for the rest of the church, both in the form of credibility and reputation. If we are experiencing issues with this today, in the 21st Century, I can only imagine the types of issues that Peter was specifically concerned with.

Just like any leadership role, Elders have been given the duty of stewardship responsibility, in which they must be accountable to Christ for how they lead. Leaders are not acquiring followers for their own benefit; instead, God is bringing followers to them.[13] It is God that is building the church, not the leaders – the leaders do the assigned tasks. Scripture throughout the New Testament lays this out clearly.

Elders are considered shepherds of souls who are accountable to the Chief Shepherd,[14] Jesus Christ, who "shall appear" at the second coming. He will judge His ministers, specifically Elders in the case of this letter, from His throne. As Peter shares in 5:4, if the Elders have been obedient and faithful to the doctrines and commands of Christ, then He will crown them in eternal glory that will not fade away. We note that the Greek word for *"fadeth not"* comes from a fabled flower known as the amaranth, which does not fade.[15]

Both Peter and Paul made references to crowns as symbols of rewards. These are not to be seen as rewards for payment of some form of human endeavor or accomplishment, but as tokens of gratitude of their faithfulness to the Lord's Kingdom; in Christ's case, faithfulness to allowing God to work through the individual. During the times of the First Century, crowns were given to people as marks of distinction, typically achievements that were extremely notable and critical to the kingdom(s) they served. We, as His children, are also promised crowns of eternal glory, life, and righteousness and our crowns will also not...*fade away.*

The expression *"God working through you"* means that you are being obedient to what God wants you to do, what He wants you to say, and how He wants you to say it (for example). God's part of the process is to give you the information you require, provide you with words of knowledge in the situation, infuse you with confidence, and charge you with the energy to get you through the tasks assigned to you. In some cases, you may also be filled with His power to perform miracles such as healing (He is doing the healing – you are the conduit of His power). Not only does the reward for faithfulness apply to the mature, but the same principle is also at work in the young, as Peter delves into in 5:5.

The interesting part of 5:5 that catches my attention every time I read it is the opening phrase of the verse *"Likewise, ye younger..."* Peter is now admonishing younger people to submit themselves to the care of their Elders. One might think that "younger" might refer to those that are simply new to the faith but the Greek Word used here, *neos*, means both "young AND new;" it also means "new self, " which may refer to new Christians regardless of age. Sequentially, the word Elders in this verse *presbuteros*, means "older" or "men of old" in addition to their spiritual authority.

Therefore, I interpret this verse as being specifically age-related[16] in that Peter was talking to younger people to submit themselves to those that are older than them as a mark of respect and honor. [*Note: I would accept, with no debate, anyone that also includes new Christians in this regard as we all ought to respect and honor those that have more experience and wisdom (not just knowledge) about things of the Holy Spirit*]. Nevertheless, the idea of being younger implies a more headstrong attitude, more resistant to leadership[17], which is why Peter was specifically calling out the youth.

Scriptures have much to say about submission – to government, to parents, to ministry leaders. Within ministry, a lack of submission makes the efforts of ministry unnecessarily difficult but, more important than the difficulties, is that those that do not submit forfeit God's grace.[18]

Perhaps Peter was advising the young that the older generations (the sages) have wisdom to share based on lessons learned in life, mistakes and achievements, so that younger generations don't have to struggle as hard, wasting time and effort in trying to bring in fresh meanings and contexts. Oh, how our generation today is losing this, now viewing the elderly in a much different way! Perhaps this is reason enough to leave history alone and stop trying to reinvent or rewrite it – the bad stuff and the good stuff. For history is where our lessons reside.

To continue, Peter, not neglecting to stress that the entire congregation needs to be held accountable because we all need help regardless of where we are "spiritually," demands that *"all of you be subject one to another."* We need people to help advise us if we are about to take a wrong turn. If we are going to allow ourselves to be corrected when necessary, we should always operate from a place of humility, which is what Peter means when he tells us to *"be clothed in humility. "*

Why do we need to be humble? Because the opposite of humility is pride and a person operating in a spirit of pride will resist correction. In turn, God will resist giving out grace to those filled with pride. A person that is humble will receive what God has for them because God *"giveth grace to the humble."* Grace both gives us the ability to lead and the heartfelt ability to obey. When referring to grace from God, Peter was likely quoting from Proverbs 3:34, which says in the KJV, *"He gives grace to the afflicted."* James puts it this way, *"God is opposed to the proud but gives grace to the humble."*

Humility, in scripture, is an attitude of showing our neediness so that God can accomplish His will through us.[19] It is mentioned throughout scripture as a posture that all people should adopt; this is the best position for the person to grow and expand. Humility is an inward response to the idea of submission and means that you are modest, or not high-minded in attitude or position. Based on the use of this word in scripture and its frequency, humility must have been as much of a challenge for people in the First Century as it is today.

I would like to close on a thought about this idea of submitting to, well, anyone, but church leaders more specifically. A church is filled with a lot of people who are hurting in some manner or fashion; it could be hurts they brought on themselves or hurts inflicted on them by others. In some cases, people have been hurt by people that they thought cared for them or would protect them, people whose care they were placed in voluntarily (think of teachers, parents, sports coaches, or other family members, for example).

In some cases, people faithfully follow the biblical mandate to submit themselves to their church leaders, but by virtue of human weakness, events follow where a person ends up being hurt by a church leader (or something more horrific such as the Catholic church scandals). Perhaps the church leader started following a doctrine that no longer aligned with scripture but according to their own convictions; when asked about it, instead of teaching the church member, the church leader's first or second response is to remind the person about the principle of submission to church leaders. This then cascades into the church member beginning to question accountability as he or she has just witnessed, firsthand, that even experienced church leaders are not immune to pride. As a result his trust and respect are eroded.

Whether hurt by a church leader or another person of ministerial authority, depending on the degree of pain, people may struggle with the idea of humbly submitting in the future, and trustfully placing themselves under the care of others as pointedly stated in scriptures such as 1 Peter 5:5. These church members will start attending a new church, one in which the Lord has, hopefully, placed them, but it may take time for trust to be earned and the pain healed before the person allows themselves to humbly submit to a leader in their new church. In some cases, it may take years.

In almost all cases of this type of past pain and trauma, there may only be an extremely tiny fraction of people who are aware of the back story. It may even be possible that leaders in the new church aren't fully aware (because they are not yet trusted). It may take time before the church member confesses and shares their pain with their new church leaders. Do you recognize this in either yourself or someone you know intimately? It happened to my wife and me and it was a horribly traumatic experience. But God's grace is always there for proper healing and reconciliation. Therefore Elders, and other church leaders, *must* take their responsibilities seriously as they can severely damage the spirit and soul of their congregants.

Church leaders are held to a higher standard of moral, ethical, and Christian behavior than others of the congregation. This behavior is developed in future church leader as he or she matures and develops spiritually and emotionally; this is also the reason why Elders must be spiritually mature and emotionally intelligent before occupying the seat of Elder. On some levels, this may not seem fair as church leaders are human and have their own issues just like everyone else; but the souls of the flock are too important to Jesus to take for granted. This is not an escape clause for normal church members concerning their behavior, but just like the military or other hierarchical style organizations, the higher up the ladder you go, the more you must be cautious of what you say and do.

Church leaders are also held to higher standards of accountability in the eyes of Jesus Christ Himself, the Chief Shepherd of all shepherds. Perhaps this is why Peter took time to deal with the topic of Elders in this section of his letter, to outline their expectations, and the reward from Jesus if they remain faithful.

15

In Conclusion, Maintain an Attitude of Submission to God while Resisting the Devil 1 Peter 5:6 - 11 (NKJV)

PREMISE

Peter is continuing with the plot of his letter by reminding his readers to remain humble and maintain their trust and faith in God with ALL of their cares. It is humility that advances us with God and with other people around us – the opposite being that we can be obstinate, arrogant, and conceited (but what would that win us?). When we are humble, God will exalt us at the right time[1], and this requires the character of patience because we don't know when "the right time" will be. Meanwhile, the devil is working overtime through multiple attempts to destroy believers like a roaring lion on the prowl. Believers are to resist him and stand firm in their faith.² When suffering comes, we must remind ourselves that we are ultimately called into the Lord's eternal glory which is found only in Christ. The devil can't touch that glory; but we can give up and lose it.

In the previous section, Peter had quoted from Proverbs 3:34. If God gives grace to the humble, it behooves believers to humble themselves before God in order to meet the requirements of this much needed grace. This section is all about the attitudes that are necessary for the Christ follower to mature and grow in Christ. These attitudes include submission, humility, trust, sober mindedness, vigilant defense, hope, worship, and faithfulness.

First Peter Chapter 5 (cont'd)

⁶ Therefore humble yourselves under the mighty hand of God, that He may exalt you in due time, ⁷ casting all your care upon Him, for He cares for you.

⁸ Be sober, be vigilant; because your adversary the devil walks about like a roaring lion, seeking whom he may devour. ⁹ Resist him, steadfast in the faith, knowing that the same sufferings are experienced by your brotherhood in the world. ¹⁰ But may the God of all grace, who called us to His eternal glory by Christ Jesus, after you have suffered a while, perfect, establish, strengthen, and settle *you.* ¹¹ To Him *be* the glory and the dominion forever and ever. Amen.

In Conclusion, Maintain an Attitude of Submission to God while Resisting the Devil

As had been mentioned in another chapter, whenever a verse of scripture begins with *"therefore,"* as in 5:6, the writer is trying to emphasize what he previously stated; in other words, he is saying "this is why what I just shared with you is important; it is there for..." You won't fully understand the verses that follow unless you understand the verses that preceded it. In this case, Peter is getting ready to share with us why his discussion about the importance of humility and the character and conduct of Elders is important.

Peter is admonishing his readers to maintain an attitude of both submission AND humility to God, not just in reference to a particular situation or an event, but in our lives as a whole. Our humble attitudes are to be demonstrated under the *"mighty hand of God,"* which is both an incentive and a reason for humility.[3] If we rely too much on ourselves, we slowly, and subtlety remove ourselves from a sense of God's sovereignty, until we ultimately find ourselves in a situation where we don't understand how we got there. This, in turn, is when we realize that it is much safer to be under God's mighty hand, and because of His sovereignty He can be trusted.[4]

"The mighty hand of God" assures us that we are always accomplishing His purpose and not our own. The Lord delivered Israel out of Egypt under His "mighty hand," so why wouldn't He do the same for you and me? Believers should not fight against God, though our flesh will fight us and, for some, this battle can be relentless. One evidence of the lack of submission and humility is impatience with

God (scripture in the New Testament often testifies that we ought to maintain an attitude of patient endurance). As with all things, the way we conduct ourselves gets easier over time as long as we remain vigilant and focused on the changes we want to experience. Ultimately, we all want to be elevated by God, but this will happen only in His time. What does it mean to you to be elevated? For some of us, we just want to live a life free of stress and anxiety, but God wants more for us. Why? So that we are equipped to share His good news.

God will lift up suffering, submissive, humble believers in His wisely appointed time.[5] That *"He may exalt you in due time"* implies that your days of humiliation will not last forever and that He will exalt you at the proper time - meaning that He will elevate or promote you, as well as glorify you and praise you. Easy to read but harder to follow in practice depending on what you are in the middle of. And then there is the idea that He will exalt you at the proper time. When is the proper time? It seems that for some people, they recover rather quickly while for others it takes a little longer. If this is you, this is when our faith can, and will, be truly tested.

I don't believe that Peter is positioning God as someone who rewards us based on some form of scale or merit system. This is ludicrous on its own merits; yet some people actually believe this. This belief will ultimately serve as a doorway to false humility and pride which are deadly to a man's faith. The believer is to be completely and wholly devoted and submitted to the Lord so that we will be glorified "in due time." This most likely refers to the return of Christ as Peter indicates in 1:5 and 2:12.[6]

Failure to humble oneself and submit to God implies the direct opposite: we are self-concerned while exalting ourselves (we worship our own efforts), which would be foolish and ill timed. The proper time to be exalted is when God decides to exalt the believer, not when the believer exalts himself or herself. Remember, patient endurance.

In 5:7, Peter is partly quoting from Psalm 55:22. *"Casting"* means to throw something on to something, such as a fishing net in the water; it also means to cast aside without regard to care or concern.[7] Peter is advising his readers to cast off all forms of negative emotion or feeling and give them to God, trusting Him with what He is doing. Casting aside such feelings as doubt, fear, discouragement, or despair, along with being humble and submissive, shows that we wholly trust God. Some commentaries state that this is one of the main characteristics of living a victorious Christian life. However, take note that this is about casting our cares and our worries, not our actions or responsibilities. Our act shows that we trust God and His promise that He truly cares for us.

> *Psalm 55:22: "Cast your burden on the LORD, And He shall sustain you; He shall never permit the righteous to be moved."*

In Matthew 6:25, Jesus told us not to be anxious about our lives and in John 14:1 He exhorts us to not let our hearts be troubled. In both verses, the answer is to place ALL of our trust and hope in God – to cast our worries aside. These two gifts mentioned in Matthew 6:25 and John 14:1, trust and hope, are free; we just need to take hold of them, and allow them to liberate us. Did I say to "just" take hold? Yes, because God's Word tells us to. Ooof! Easy, right?

We suffer anxiety when it seems to us that things we are comfortable with, or have gotten comfortable with, are being threatened. Oftentimes, too, we suffer anxiety when our pride or our ego have been threatened. The only solution is to simply cast aside anxiety. Right? However, we can't just "cast anxiety aside" unless we know that someone else, who we trust, is going to help us through the situation.[8] *"He cares for you,"* meaning God, is a literal statement and translation.

Most people automatically defer to the definition of "anxious" that means to worry about an imminent event or something with an uncertain outcome. But "anxious" also means to want something very much, typically with a feeling of restlessness (eager, desirous, impatience, longing). In either case, being anxious is living with anxiety.

> "I am eager to stop being anxious. I strongly long for that, but this desire is making me anxious."

Some people have mastered the art of being anxious, while others have mastered the exact opposite (restful, untroubled, quiet). Anxious people look at these other people and envy them, which is another sin that causes further anxiety. But most people fall in the middle, anxious at moments, restful at others.

> "Don't you worry?"
> "Would it help?"
> ~ Bridge of Spies (2015), starring Tom Hanks

Can you be true to yourself and honest, about where you are regarding this tendency to be anxious? How capable are you of casting all, or at least some, of your cares and worries to God?

It can be argued that as long as you are making all of the right choices and have planned accordingly, then there is no reason for you to be anxious about anything.[9] However, if we have made all of the right choices and planned accordingly, our new challenge is the concern we have about the "choices of others," and how the decisions of others may impact us – this is cause for anxiety. We may worry about others' choices and/or we may wait in eager anticipation for them to make a decision.

In our hearts we pray that we make the right choices, but we also pray that others make the right choices as well. It becomes personal when the choices of others impact us. Why? Because we have opinions about what the right choices are that align with the values that are part of "our" belief system. When someone makes a choice that does not align with our value system, and it either directly or indirectly impacts us, this can cause anxiety. But it doesn't have to.

Thank God for His grace and His strength, else, what else do you have in your arsenal that you can use to move forward when anxiety rears its ugly head? Just make a choice to "not worry about it" and cast all of your worries to God. Easy for some, more difficult for others.

In verse 5:8, Peter begins to touch on the area of preparation in the form of a warning. Just because Christ followers believe in the sovereignty of God does not mean that we can live careless and carefree lives; we must always remain alert against outside forces that seek to influence, distract, mislead or misdirect us.[10] The Greek word for devil, *diabolos,* means "false accuser" or "slanderer;" he is an enemy who wants to defame and smear believers. The devil's existence is only one part of the reality of playing the game of life on earth; the other part is ourselves and our response to situations. Nonetheless, verse 5:8 is one of those verses that is not necessarily focused on the sin of pride as much as it is focused on the one who seduces you and wants you to yield to pride,[11] thereby replacing your dependence on God with your own individual pride. This creates conflict, not just within yourself but with others as well. Wars have started because of this.

However, unlike God, the devil is neither omnipresent nor omniscient, which means that the other reality of the game of life is to recognize that he can't be in multiple places or times all at once. I believe that some of us forget this and tend to give way too much credit to the devil when, in reality, we are causing or creating our own negative situations. Or we are simply being tempted and call it "an attack of the devil," when it is really us fighting ourselves. The devil may have created pornography, but he isn't necessarily the one getting inside of your head and telling you to watch it and then...sin. That is most likely all you; however, the devil and his demons are looking for opportunities to overwhelm you, persecute you, and discourage you.

To *"be sober"* means that we need to be realistic about our natural tendency to think that we can either take care of it ourselves, or fears we have about our abilities, or fear that God won't be there for you when you need Him.[12] As we see in Paul's remarks in Romans

12:3, true humility is not making ourselves something less than we are or demoting ourselves, but it is acknowledging God's gifts and how these gifts work in and through us – for we have all received a standard or measurement of faith.

> Romans 12:3: "For I say, through the grace given to me, to everyone who is among you, not to think of himself more highly than he ought to think, but to think soberly, as God has dealt to each one a measure of faith."

As we survey and evaluate ourselves, we should take time to recognize and give thanks for what God has accomplished in us (i.e., faith), not the things that we think we did ourselves. The other area to survey and evaluate is the ability that God has given us, by His grace, to resist the things of the devil.

The devil is hungry for opportunities to accuse God to men, to accuse men to God before God's throne, and to accuse men amongst other men.[13] The devil has definitely gotten a foothold in American culture recently, accusing God to men, and accusing men amongst men. He will do things, or create systems and tools, to drag and pull Christ followers out of Christian service or from the Christian lifestyle. The devil wants to convince you to abandon God or to make you believe that God has abandoned you. The good news is that God will not abandon you – He can't because He said that He will never leave us nor forsake us? (Hebrews 13:5).

So, this means that we must be "spiritually vigilant" while keeping our minds, eyes, and ears on the alert for the bait that the devil puts out. Peter has given us the image of the lion to draw a picture of the threat he is to us. It is satan who is roaring and prowling, searching for Christ followers who he can terrify in the middle of the night or in the midst of a struggle so that they will be deceived and fall (or worse, backslide completely, which implies that they have abandoned God). Notice how both the devil, and Jesus, are referred to as a lion in scripture. The devil is nowhere near as powerful as the Lion of Judah, but he is smart and he knows how to disguise himself.

The second layer of good news is that He will equip you with the power necessary to firmly resist and defeat the devil. All you have to say is "Devil, shut up," or "Get out of here," or shrug him off with the ever famous "Whatever, dude!" All you have to do is "walk away," or "close that browser," or "delete that email." Resist! Simple, right?

In verse 5:9, Peter tells us to resist the devil. To "resist" means to oppose or stand up against. The truth is, no matter what anyone says, there is no "magic formula" or "bible secret" to resisting the devil – it is 100% about you standing fast on your faith in the knowledge of who you are, who God is, and who you are in God. That's it. If you are doing anything, believing anything, or saying anything that tears or takes you down, you need to start telling yourself a different story. It's the story that you are telling yourself that is taking you down and the way out of that pit is to reclaim the truth of who you are in Christ. Now start telling that story right and climb your way out of that pit to the peak above.

The ability to resist implies that you have been living, and continue to live, your life according to the Word of God[14]; which further implies that you are spending personal time in...you guessed it...the Word of God. And this is one the most dominant areas in hurting men today. If you aren't spending personal time meditating on God's Word, how do you know how to stand your ground on the faith apportioned to you by God? It is only as we come to know God's truth that we can obey His truth and withstand satan.

The final area, for what it's worth (which is a lot), is the knowledge that whatever you are going through is not unique to you. Someone else has already experienced the same thing, is currently experiencing the same thing, or is (or has) experiencing things that are significantly worse and more dramatic than what you are going through. This verse doesn't specifically say it, but there is added comfort in the knowledge that others have already gotten through the same struggle you are experiencing, or they have gotten through struggles that are worse than that. If you have awareness of this, it adds to your hope – believe it! Easy to say, harder to live by; but that is why we have faith. Either way, some of our fellow Christians are living examples that suffering is only temporary, even if it sucks while going through it.

There is absolutely no need to be afraid of satan. The Lord has equipped us with everything we need to resist and stand against him, but this does, as mentioned earlier, require that we stand firm in our faith. It is our trust in God's promises that allows us to see that suffering is not the final outcome and that we will, as already noted in 5:6, be exalted.

While in the middle of some form of sufferings, a final truth is that even though other Christians are experiencing the same thing, not every believer is experiencing the exact same degree of tribulation,[15] meaning the burden doesn't seem to be as harsh on some as it is on others. It doesn't always seem fair. Nevertheless, this doesn't preclude believers from standing firm in their faith about God's promises.

Sometimes, we can get so caught up in the comparison trap, that we fail to see where the variables are different, or we simply don't know all of the variables. In fact, carrying this truth a little deeper, some Christians may seem to have completely escaped the "trial," even though everything seems to point to the idea that they should be suffering. Why are they appearing to survive while you aren't? The answer is that there are variables that are always different. Perhaps it has something to do with how they prepare, how they spend time with God and His Word when things are peaceful.

Peter moves on into verse 5:10 about God's grace. One of the concepts that modern day Christians may have challenges with is that some, or a lot, of God's purposes won't be known until the future – and, in some cases, that future may be when we are standing in front of Him (after we have died). Peter wants his readers to know that, when suffering, we should continue to live our lives in a way that the grace of God is still manifesting in us[16] (a close and continuing reference to 4:6). His grace didn't suddenly stop just because it seems like it.

Making this verse even more "interesting" is the idea that we are being perfected by the Lord right in the middle of our trial, in real time as we are "suffering." Verse 5:10 includes four verbs, that, while differing somewhat based on the translation you are reading, represent the impact that God's grace has on you while under this "attack." *"After you have suffered a while,"* God will **perfect** you, **establish** you, **strengthen** you, and **settle** you.[17] We are reminded that God will, at some point, restore whatever we have lost for the sake of Christ. Bottom line is that God is trying to produce strength of character in you and will honor His believers who suffered as a result of faith in Him on earth.

- "Perfecting" pertains to the furthering of our sanctification.
- "Establishing" brings us into consistent Christian Living.
- "Strengthening" refers to spiritual power.
- "Settling" means that we are gaining confidence in our salvation.

One of the most difficult things for a modern Westernized (industrialized) Christian to realize is that we have no idea how long until Christ returns. We can tend to be spoiled and overly comfortable with life as compared to our brothers and sisters who live in less developed, prosperous nations (Third World) – or in areas where Christianity is disapproved of such as China or the Middle East. For some, this reality is still difficult to swallow when we consider the truth that from God's perspective, our time on earth is a blip on the radar. As a result, if you can wrap your mind around it, the amount of time we suffer is nothing when compared to a future life in eternity. (c.f., Romans 8:17-18, 2 Corinthians 4:16-18).

Peter finishes this section of his letter in 5:11 with a short benediction about the ultimate goal of God,[18] which acknowledges His supremacy. Christ followers have nothing to fear because God is sovereign over everyone and everything. God is supreme now, but, as many theologians agree, God is allowing history to play itself out.

Your choice is to believe, or not to believe. But I have a question: which decision involves the greatest risk?

16

The Grand Finale: Farewell and Peace
1 Peter 5:12 - 14 (AMP)

PREMISE

This is it, the finale of Peter's letter. There isn't much that can be said of Silvanus, a figure familiar to those who read Scripture. He was an associate of the two most popular apostles of the time, Paul and Peter. He was also called Silas and is believed to have both composed and delivered Peter's first letter, the one we have been studying in this book.

Peter closes out his letter with a benediction and a call for peace by reminding believers to stand firm in the true grace of God. He chooses to make references to a woman in Babylon as part of his final greeting, a statement that is most likely about the church in Rome, as

215

a final reminder that all believers are Christian exiles who will eventually receive the inheritance as promised by God.

This closing benediction is an appropriate ending to the letter because, even while Christians are being persecuted on earth, heaven's peace cannot be taken from them. Suffering is the theme of this letter, but the letter also shows that grace is brought in as the means by which believers survive and carry themselves through the suffering they endure.

First Peter Chapter 5 (cont'd)

[12] By Silvanus, our faithful brother (as I consider him), I have written to you briefly, to counsel and testify that this is the true grace [the undeserved favor] of God. Stand firm in it! [13] She [the church] who is in Babylon, chosen together with you, sends you greetings, and *so does* my son [in the faith], Mark. [14] Greet one another with a kiss of love.

To all of you who are in Christ, may there be peace.

The Grand Finale: Farewell and Peace

In 5:12, we are finally introduced to Silvanus, a prophet and a Roman citizen (see Acts 16:37), also known as Silas. Silas was Paul's travel companion on his second missionary journey as written about in Acts Chapter 15[1]; he was also the secretary who is believed to have helped Peter compose this letter. The Amplified begins with the words *"Through Silvanus"* in 5:12, whereas the King James uses the words *"By Silvanus."* The original Greek word used here is *Dia,* which refers to "motion" or "on account of." Therefore, not only did Silvanus compose the letter, but I agree with most theologians, that he also delivered it. The letter was completed and delivered "on account of" Silvanus.

However, it's worth mentioning that, even though the letter is credited to Peter, some theologians argue that Silvanus may actually have interjected some of his own thoughts. This conclusion is drawn due to differences in writing style and vocabulary choices between First Peter and Second Peter. As Silvanus physically wrote the letter, it is possible that he included his own vocabulary and thoughts in the letter;[2] however, Peter would have read the letter before Silvanus departed with it, so we can safely presume that the letter was approved by Peter as led and guided by the Holy Spirit.

Peter concludes in 5:12 by affirming that the letter was testified, delivered, and written, by *"the true grace of God"* and further emphasizing that Christians must "stand firm" on the faith of God even in the middle of persecution and suffering.[3] Christian life can be summarized as consisting of the grace of God who has provided salvation and is actively and currently working salvation in all believers.

Many commentators suggest that grace is the primary theme of this letter. I, however, agree with those that believe that the expectation of suffering is the overriding theme and problem presented in the letter, but grace is brought in as the solution/answer to how believers survive[4] and conduct themselves through the suffering they endure – all due to the glory of God.

What follows in the last two verses of the letter (5:13-14) is a parting farewell which includes phraseology that is somewhat cryptic, *"She who is in Babylon."* I believe this is a reference to the church in Rome, as shown in the Amplified version; however, there are some that believe this is a literal reference to a woman, possibly Peter's wife.[5] I believe it is a reference to the Church in Rome with 1 John 1 and 13 serving as other scriptural examples of where the church and its congregants were referred to in the female gender.

Babylon, a reference to the Old Testament city in Mesopotamia, was already in ruins at the time this letter was written, but because of Israel's tumultuous history with Babylon, the reference to the city represented opposition to God as well as a place of exile. At the time Peter was writing his letter, it would have been a common metaphor for Rome (First Century Rome symbolized the Old Testament Babylon). Babylon in the New Testament context would have a notorious connotation because of the violence and atrocities that Israel suffered in its history at the hands of Babylonians. Those of the Christian faith, including Gentile converts, would have recognized Babylon/Rome as a place where Christians were living as exiles but who would later receive the inheritance as promised and guaranteed by God.

The Mark mentioned at the end of 5:13 is the same Mark who wrote the Gospel of Mark, who many believe was aided by Peter in many accounts. He is also the same Mark who traveled with Paul and Barnabas during their first missionary journey[6] as described in the Book of Acts. He left Barnabas and Paul during that journey (due to a falling out) but was later restored by key members of the church (see

Colossians 4:10, 2 Timothy 4:11, Philemon 1:24). Peter would have become familiar with Mark during the earliest days of the church when they were meeting in his mother's house (see Acts 12:12). Peter and Mark would have grown close over the years, where Peter would eventually become Mark's spiritual mentor and spiritual father.

It was the custom in most letters and epistles of the New Testament to refer to many figures popular in the church at the time who, considering the size of the Roman Empire, would have been well known to believers. This is another reason it is not likely that it was Peter's wife being referenced alongside Mark in this letter.

The reference to greeting *"one another with a kiss of love"* in the final verse of the letter is similar to a *"holy kiss"* as found in other passages of scripture such as Romans 16:16, 1 Corinthians 16:20, and 1 Thessalonians 5:26. This was the custom of the day and would be equivalent to the modern day "church hug."[7] Peter's final words as he closes the letter are a final prayer and benediction towards peace, even while suffering, which readers can expect because they are in Christ and receive the grace of God.

Appendix: Endnotes

Note: Endnote references to study bibles are compiled from their commentary notes.

CHAPTER 1

1. Peter was the bridge to James for the Church (https://en.wikipedia.org/wiki/Saint_Peter)
2. Debate about epistle authorship: William Baker - "*The Books of James and Peter*" pg. 96; ESV Study Bible pg. 2401; NASB Study Bible pg 1905
3. Book likely written between 60-64 AD: CSB Study Bible pg. 1974; ESV Study Bible pg. 2401; NASB Study Bible pg. 1905
4. Peters contribution to the Gospel of Mark: (https://en.wikipedia.org/wiki/Saint_Peter), (https://overviewbible.com/apostle-peter)
5. Eusibius contribution to the story of the Apostle Peter: (https://overviewbible.com/apostle-peter)
6. Flavius Josephus contribution to the story of the early Church: (https://en.wikipedia.org/wiki/Josephus)

CHAPTER 2

1. Book likely written between 60-64 AD: CSB Study Bible pg. 1974; ESV Study Bible pg. 2401; NASB Study Bible pg. 1905
2. Peters crucifixion: NASB Study Bible pg. 1905; (https://en.wikipedia.org/wiki/Saint_Peter), (https://overviewbible.com/apostle-peter)
3. Emperors Domitian (81-96 AD) and Trajan (98-117 AD): ESV Study Bible pg. 2401
4. Scholars that question Peter's authorship: ESV Study Bible pg. 2401; CSB Study Bible pg. 1974; NASB Study Bible pg. 1905
5. Peter wrote to struggling believers: William Baker - "*The Books of James and Peter*" pg. 96-97; CSB Study Bible pg. 1973-1975; NASB Study Bible pg. 1905-1907; ESV Study Bible pg. 2401-2403
6. "...a Christian can evangelize his hostile world.": NASB Study Bible pg. 1906
7. Quote attributed to Martin Luther: compiled from William Baker - "*The Books of James and Peter*" pg. 95

8. Book written to Gentiles: ESV Study Bible pg. 2402; CSB Study Bible pg. 1974
9. Quote attributed to Simon Kistermaker: compiled from William Baker - "*The Books of James and Peter*" pg. 95
10. Doctrine of Faith: William Baker - "*The Books of James and Peter*" pg. 98; ESV Study Bible pg. 2402-2403

CHAPTER 3

1. God is the author of our salvation: William Baker - "*The Books of James and Peter*" pg. 101;
2. Peter was among a unique group of men: NASB Study Bible pg. 1908
3. Converted Jews: NASB Study Bible pg. 1905; William Baker - "*The Books of James and Peter*" pg. 95-96
4. Christians and Israel: William Baker - "*The Books of James and Peter*" pg. 102; ESV Study Bible pg. 2405
5. Elect/Chosen (*elektos*): NKJV Study Bible pg. 1692; NASB Study Bible pg. 1908
6. Scattered/Dispersed: CSB Study Bible pg. 1976
7. Foreknowledge and a believers election: William Baker - "*The Books of James and Peter*" pg. 101-102; NASB Study Bible pg. 1908; ESV Study Bible pg. 1976
8. God did not reject Israel: William Baker - "*The Books of James and Peter*" pg. 102;
9. Fore-loved: William Baker - "*The Books of James and Peter*" pg. 102-103
10. Foreknowledge also means that God pre-planned a believers salvation: NASB Study Bible pg. 1908
11. Predestination: (https://en.wikipedia.org/wiki/Predestination)
12. Set apart: NASB Study Bible pg. 1908
13. Sanctification "to make holy": William Baker - "*The Books of James and Peter*" pg. 103
14. Getting to heaven: William Baker - "*The Books of James and Peter*" pg. 103
15. Cannot separate sanctification from obedience: CSB Study Bible pg. 1976; William Baker - "*The Books of James and Peter*" pg. 103; NASB Study Bible pg. 1908
16. You cannot obey Christ and separate from people: NASB Study Bible pg. 1908; William Baker - "*The Books of James and Peter*" pg. 103
17. Sprinkled with the blood of Jesus: NASB Study Bible pg. 1908; ESV Study Bible pg. 2405
18. Grace and peace: William Baker - "*The Books of James and Peter*" pg. 103

19. Caused us to be born again: ESV Study Bible pg. 2405; NASB Study Bible pg. 1908
20. Mercy and grace: William Baker - "*The Books of James and Peter*" pg. 104; ESV Study Bible pg. 2405
21. Living Hope of Jesus Christ: NASB Study Bible pg. 1908
22. Inheritance as a child of God: William Baker - "*The Books of James and Peter*" pg. 105
23. Heavenly inheritance: NASB Study Bible pg. 1908
24. God's protection: ESV Study Bible pg. 2405
25. The "last time": William Baker - "*The Books of James and Peter*" pg. 106
26. No one can steal your inheritance: NASB Study Bible pg. 1908-1909
27. Greatly rejoice: William Baker - "*The Books of James and Peter*" pg. 106
28. Trials and trouble: NASB Study Bible pg. 1909
29. Prove their faith: William Baker - "*The Books of James and Peter*" pg. 106
30. God doesn't need proof of faith: William Baker - "*The Books of James and Peter*" pg. 106; ESV Study Bible pg. 2405-2406; NASB Study Bible pg. 1909
31. Great joy: William Baker - "*The Books of James and Peter*" pg. 107; ESV Study Bible pg. 2406
32. Obtaining salvation: NASB Study Bible, pg. 1909
33. Old Testament prophets searched and inquired: William Baker - "*The Books of James and Peter*" pg. 108; ESV Study Bible pg. 2406
34. OT prophets were not serving themselves: William Baker - "*The Books of James and Peter*" pg. 108; NASB Study Bible pg. 1909

CHAPTER 4

1. Fear God's judgement: William Baker - "*The Books of James and Peter*" pg. 111; ESV Study Bible pg. 2406
2. Inheritance of grace: CSB Study Bible pg. 1976
3. Call to Action: William Baker - "*The Books of James and Peter*" pg. 111
4. Be ready for anything: NASB Study Bible pg. 1909; William Baker - "*The Books of James and Peter*" pg. 111
5. "Gird up" before battle: NASB Study Bible pg. 1909
6. Keep minds dominated on the Word of God: Rick Renner - "Spiritual Gems I" pg. 396, 445
7. The "loins" of our mind: Rick Renner - "Spiritual Gems I" pg. 396, 445
8. "keep sober *in spirit*", "*in spirit*" not in original text: William Baker - "*The Books of James and Peter*" pg. 111

9. Steadfastness, self-control, clarity of mind...: NASB Study Bible pg. 1909

10. Completion of our salvation: NASB Study Bible pg. 1909; CSB Study Bible pg. 1976; William Baker - "*The Books of James and Peter*" pg. 111-112

11. We live according to God's standards of morality: William Baker - "*The Books of James and Peter*" pg. 112; ESV Study Bible pg. 2406;

12. Apostle Paul's take on the human conscience: William Baker - "*The Books of James and Peter*" pg. 112

13. Spiritual common sense: Rick Renner - "Spiritual Gems II" pg. 652

14. God's expectations of holiness: ESV Study Bible pg. 2406; William Baker - "*The Books of James and Peter*" pg. 112; NASB Study Bible pg. 1909-1910; CSB Study Bible pg. 1976

15. Fear God and His judgement: ESV Study Bible pg. 2406; CSB Study Bible pg. 1976

16. "God's tenderness and love": quote attributed to CSB Study Bible pg. 1976

17. Redeemed from the curse of the law: ESV Study Bible pg. 2406; NASB Study Bible pg. 191018

18. Our past life had no future: William Baker - "*The Books of James and Peter*" pg. 11219

19. Jesus Christ in the trinity: William Baker - "*The Books of James and Peter*" pg. 113

20. Jesus was "foreknown": ESV Study Bible pg. 2407; NASB Study Bible pg. 1910; CSB Study Bible pg. 1977

21. Belief in God: William Baker - "*The Books of James and Peter*" pg. 113

22. God provided us with salvation in Christ: CSB Study Bible pg. 1977; William Baker - "*The Books of James and Peter*" pg. 113;

23. Love the brotherhood, no matter what: CSB Study Bible pg. 1977

24. Born again by the seed of God: William Baker - "*The Books of James and Peter*" pg. 114; ESV Study Bible pg. 2406-2407; NASB Study Bible pg. 1910

25. Merging the New Gospel Message with the Old Testament: ESV Study Bible pg. 2407

26. Evil exhibited by a person, not satan: NASB Study Bible pg. 1910;

27. 1 Peter CH 1 should continue to verse 2:3: William Baker - "*The Books of James and Peter*" pg. 114

28. Sins that disrupt the Church: William Baker - "*The Books of James and Peter*" pg. 114

29. Spiritual hunger for the Word should become intense: William Baker - "*The Books of James and Peter*" pg. 114-115

30. Spiritual growth increases: NASB Study Bible pg. 1911

CHAPTER 5

1. Jesus as the Living Stone: William Baker - "*The Books of James and Peter*" pg. 119; NASB Study Bible pg. 1911
2. We come to Jesus as living stones: William Baker - "*The Books of James and Peter*" pg. 119
3. The Living Stone as a paradox: NASB Study Bible pg. 1911
4. Christ rejection led to His Church: William Baker - "*The Books of James and Peter*" pg. 120; ESV Study Bible pg. 2407
5. Spiritual household: NASB Study Bible pg. 1911; ESV Study Bible pg. 2407; CSB Study Bible pg. 1977
6. Spiritual sacrifices: William Baker - "*The Books of James and Peter*" pg. 120; ESV Study Bible pg. 2407; NASB Study Bible pg. 1911
7. All believers in place: NASB Study Bible pg. 11
8. No formal priesthood: William Baker - "*The Books of James and Peter*" pg. 120
9. Privileges of being a priest: NASB Study Bible pg. 1911
10. Messiah who is the cornerstone: William Baker - "*The Books of James and Peter*" pg. 120; ESV Study Bible pg. 2407;
11. Stumbling over the truth: ESV Study Bible pg. 2408
12. *Skandalon*: Rick Renner - "Spiritual Gems I" pg. 327
13. Unbelievers are doomed: William Baker - "*The Books of James and Peter*" pg. 120
14. Doctrine of Reprobation: (https://en.wikipedia.org/wiki/Reprobation)
15. Doctrine of Predestination: (https://en.wikipedia.org/wiki/Predestination)
16. Believers as a chosen race: NASB Study Bible pg. 1911; ESV Study Bible pg. 2408
17. Similarities/Dissimilarities between the Church and Israel: William Baker - "*The Books of James and Peter*" pg. 121
18. Some come to have faith: William Baker - "*The Books of James and Peter*" pg. 122; NASB Study Bible pg. 1911
19. View life as a stranger, citizen, or servant: NASB Study Bible pg. 1911

CHAPTER 6

1. Submission that silences ignorant and foolish men: CSB Bible Study pg. 1978; William Baker - "*The Books of James and Peter*" pg. 125; ESV Study Bible pg. 2408
2. Submission when authority is abused: William Baker - "*The Books of James and Peter*" pg. 125; NASB Study Bible pg. 1912

3. God's law and man's law: William Baker - "*The Books of James and Peter*" pg. 126; NASB Study Bible pg. 1912

4. Maintain a godly testimony: William Baker - "*The Books of James and Peter*" pg. 126; ESV Study Bible pg. 2408

5. We submit for God's sake: NASB Study Bible pg. 1912; William Baker - "*The Books of James and Peter*" pg. 126

6. Purpose of government: ESV Study Bible pg. 2408; William Baker - "*The Books of James and Peter*" pg. 126; NASB Study Bible pg. 1912

7. Government will trend towards an anti-Christ system: William Baker - "*The Books of James and Peter*" pg. 126-127

8. First Century Christians classified as anarchists: William Baker - "*The Books of James and Peter*" pg. 127

9. Do not misuse freedom that results from our salvation: William Baker - "*The Books of James and Peter*" pg. 127; ESV Study Bible pg. 2408; NASB Study Bible pg. 1912

10. Honor and respect ALL men: ESV Study Bible pg. 2408; William Baker - "*The Books of James and Peter*" pg. 127

11. Love Christian brothers as well as unbelievers: ESV Study Bible pg. 2408

CHAPTER 7

1. We do what Jesus did: William Baker - "*The Books of James and Peter*" pg. 129; ESV Study Bible pg. 2408; NASB Study Bible pg. 1913; CSB Study Bible pg. 1978

2. Slavery references in Scripture and the world: William Baker - "*The Books of James and Peter*" pg. 130

3. Patient endurance: ESV Study Bible pg. 2409

4. Some "masters" want you to retaliate: William Baker - "*The Books of James and Peter*" pg. 130-131

5. Jesus never sinned - ever!: ESV Study Bible pg. 2409; William Baker - "*The Books of James and Peter*" pg. 131-132; NASB Study Bible pg. 1913

6. The three study bibles and the books I relied on when writing this book shared inconsistencies about the idea of healing. When scripture says that "we are healed", is it spiritual healing or physical healing?: William Baker - "*The Books of James and Peter*" pg. 132; NASB Study Bible pg. 1912-1913; ESV Study Bible pg. 2409; Rick Renner - "Spiritual Gems I" pg. 261

7. Jesus as the Shepherd and Guardian: William Baker - "*The Books of James and Peter*" pg. 133; NASB Study Bible pg. 1913

CHAPTER 8

1. Wives submit to husbands: William Baker - "*The Books of James and Peter*" pg. 135; ESV Study Bible pg. 2409; CSB Study Bible pg. 1978
2. Peter's advice to wives is unique: William Baker - "*The Books of James and Peter*" pg. 135
3. The family and the local church, submission to the social order of things: NASB Study Bible pg. 1913
4. Women are not inferior to men: NASB Study Bible pg. 1913
5. Marriage between believers: William Baker - "*The Books of James and Peter*" pg. 135-136; ESV Study Bible pg. 2409
6. The idea of wives having a different religion than husbands: ESV Study Bible pg. 2409; William Baker - "*The Books of James and Peter*" pg. 136
7. Not suggesting that wives leave unbelieving husbands: ESV Study Bible pg. 2409; NASB Study Bible pg. 1913
8. A quiet wife does not mean a silent wife: ESV Study Bible pg. 2409; NASB Study Bible pg. 1913; William Baker - "*The Books of James and Peter*" pg. 136
9. Some wives may have gone beyond teachings: William Baker - "*The Books of James and Peter*" pg. 136
10. Inner beauty and outer beauty: ESV Study Bible pg. 2409; NASB Study Bible pg. 1913; William Baker - "*The Books of James and Peter*" pg. 136-137
11. Sarah refers to Abraham as "my lord": ESV Study Bible pg. 2409; William Baker - "*The Books of James and Peter*" pg. 137
12. Spiritual kin of Sarah: William Baker - "*The Books of James and Peter*" pg. 137
13. Husbands submit to Christ: ESV Study Bible pg. 2409; NASB Study Bible pg. 1913
14. Wives understand husbands more than the other way around: William Baker - "*The Books of James and Peter*" pg. 139; NASB Study Bible pg. 1913-1914; ESV Study Bible pg. 2409-2410
15. Husbands are to be sensitive to wives needs: NASB Study Bible pg. 1913-1914; ESV Study Bible pg. 2409-2410
16. The woman is equal to the husband intellectually and spiritually: NASB Study Bible pg. 1913-1914; William Baker - "*The Books of James and Peter*" pg. 138-139
17. The covenant of marriage and the Church: William Baker - "*The Books of James and Peter*" pg. 139; NASB Study Bible pg. 1913-1914

CHAPTER 9

1. Human relationships at the core: CSB Study Bible pg. 1978-1979
2. The five virtues: Rick Renner - "Spiritual Gems I" pg. 766-772
3. Christian commitment: William Baker - "*The Books of James and Peter*" pg. 141; ESV Study Bible pg. 2410
4. Virtues prevent the devil from getting into "open doors": Rick Renner - "Spiritual Gems I" pg. 766-772
5. A gentle answer: ESV Study Bible pg. 2410; William Baker - "*The Books of James and Peter*" pg. 142
6. We are not to return evil for evil, but be a blessing: William Baker - "*The Books of James and Peter*" pg. 142; ESV Study Bible pg. 2410; NASB Study Bible pg. 1914
7. Undeserved blessing instead of judgment: NASB Study Bible pg. 1914
8. Jesus never fully experienced the blessings He taught: William Baker - "*The Books of James and Peter*" pg. 142
9. Keep tongue from evil and do good: ESV Study Bible pg. 2410
10. We don't know how many times God has protected us: William Baker - "*The Books of James and Peter*" pg. 143
11. God's grace "*strengthens and establishes*": ESV Study Bible pg. 2410
12. Believers are spared much more frequently than others: William Baker - "*The Books of James and Peter*" pg. 144

CHAPTER 10

1. Suffer for righteousness: William Baker - "*The Books of James and Peter*" pg. 147
2. Christ died to bring us to the Father: William Baker - "*The Books of James and Peter*" pg. 147, 149
3. Maintain a good conscience: ESV Study Bible pg. 2410; William Baker - "*The Books of James and Peter*" pg. 148
4. 3:19-21 touted as difficult to interpret: CSB Study Bible pg. 1979; William Baker - "*The Books of James and Peter*" pg. 151
5. Peter is almost contradictory in 3:13: William Baker - "*The Books of James and Peter*" pg. 147
6. We are blessed to suffer for righteousness: CSB Study Bible pg. 1979
7. Face your detractors with the fear of God: William Baker - "*The Books of James and Peter*" pg. 147
8. Fear of God over fear of man: William Baker - "*The Books of James and Peter*" pg. 148; CSB Study Bible pg. 1979
9. To sanctify means to make holy: William Baker - "*The Books of James and Peter*" pg. 148
10. *See note 9*

11. Defense/*apologia*/apologetics: William Baker - "*The Books of James and Peter*" pg. 148
12. Remain gentle and courteous: NASB Study Bible pg. 1915; CSB Study Bible 1979
13. Maintain a good conscience: NASB Study Bible pg. 1915; ESAV Study Bible pg. 2410; William Baker - "*The Books of James and Peter*" pg. 148-149
14. Accusers shame of their own conscience: NASB Study Bible pg. 1915; ESV Study Bible pg. 2410
15. Old Testament blessings and New Testament blessings: William Baker - "*The Books of James and Peter*" pg. 149
16. Doctrine of the Cross: NASB Study Bible pg. 1914; William Baker - "*The Books of James and Peter*" pg. 149-150; CSB Study Bible pg. 1979; (https://en.wikipedia.org/wiki/Theology_of_the_Cross)
17. Doctrine of grace: NASB Study Bible pg. 1914
18. "The just for the unjust": NASB Study Bible pg. 1914; William Baker - "*The Books of James and Peter*" pg. 149
19. Not possible for Jesus to die in His divinity: William Baker - "*The Books of James and Peter*" pg. 150
20. *See note 4*
21. Study Bibles debate "spirits in prison": NASB Study Bible pg. 1914-1915; ESV Study Bible pg. 2410-2411; CSB Study Bible 1979 (this endnote applies to this entire section about the "spirits in prison")
22. The Ark that Noah built: NASB Study Bible pg. 1915
23. Saved through the water, comparing the flood and baptism: William Baker - "*The Books of James and Peter*" pg. 153; ESV Study Bible pg. 2411; NASB Study Bible pg. 1915; CSB Study Bible 1979
24. *See note 23*
25. An appeal to God: William Baker - "*The Books of James and Peter*" pg. 153-154

CHAPTER 11

1. Jesus walked the earth in the flesh: William Baker - "*The Books of James and Peter*" pg. 155; ESV Study Bible pg. 2411; NASB Study Bible pg. 1915; CSB Study Bible pg. 1980
2. Believers can cease to sin just like Jesus: William Baker - "*The Books of James and Peter*" pg. 155-156; CSB Study Bible pg. 1980; ESV Study Bible, pg. 2411
3. Believers are dead *with* Christ: William Baker - "*The Books of James and Peter*" pg. 156
4. We've wasted enough time already: William Baker - "*The Books of James and Peter*" pg. 156

5. Unlawful and unrestrained sexual activity: William Baker - "*The Books of James and Peter*" pg. 156; NASB Study Bible pg. 1915

6. Even unbelievers have spiritual instincts: William Baker - "*The Books of James and Peter*" pg. 157

7. Those who die before the Day of Judgement: William Baker - "*The Books of James and Peter*" pg. 157; ESV Study Bible pg. 2411; NASB Study Bible pg. 1915-1916; CSB Study Bible pg. 1980

8. Message preached to those who are "now" dead: William Baker - "*The Books of James and Peter*" pg. 157; ESV Study Bible pg. 2411; NASB Study Bible pg. 1916; CSB Study Bible pg. 1980; NKJV Study Bible pg. 1696

9. Believers response to repentance, forgiveness, and faith: William Baker - "*The Books of James and Peter*" pg. 157-158; ESV Study Bible pg. 2411; NASB Study Bible pg. 1916; CSB Study Bible pg. 1980

CHAPTER 12

1. How believers ought to live: William Baker - "*The Books of James and Peter*" pg. 159; ESV Study Bible pg. 2411; NASB Study Bible pg. 1916; CSB Study Bible pg. 1980

2. Above anything, remain in a position of love of others: ESV Study Bible pg. 2411; NASB Study Bible pg. 1916; CSB Study Bible pg. 1980; William Baker - "*The Books of James and Peter*" pg. 159

3. Love is an act that God can command: William Baker - "*The Books of James and Peter*" pg. 160; NASB Study Bible pg. 1916

4. Forgive those that cause problems: William Baker - "*The Books of James and Peter*" pg. 160

5. Believers are to be hospitable: William Baker - "*The Books of James and Peter*" pg. 160; ESV Study Bible pg. 2411; NASB Study Bible pg. 1916; CSB Study Bible pg. 1980

6. Gifts from God: William Baker - "*The Books of James and Peter*" pg. 160-161; ESV Study Bible pg. 2412; NASB Study Bible pg. 1916; CSB Study Bible pg. 1980

7. Gifts not to be confused with abilities learned in training: NASB Study Bible pg. 1916

8. The Apostle Paul also discussed God's special gifts: Rick Renner - "Spiritual Gems II" pg. 705-706, 893-894; William Baker - "*The Books of James and Peter*" pg. 160-161; ESV Study Bible pg. 2412; NASB Study Bible pg. 1916

9. Stewardship of God's gifts: Rick Renner - "Spiritual Gems II" pg. 705-706, 893-894; NASB Study Bible pg. 1916

10. Speak in a way that glorifies God: William Baker - "*The Books of James and Peter*" pg. 161

CHAPTER 13

1. Don't be surprised by fiery ordeals: William Baker - "*The Books of James and Peter*" pg. 163; ESV Study Bible pg. 2412
2. Four necessary attitudes: NASB Study Bible pg. 1916
3. How unbelievers react to a life of salvation through Christ: William Baker - "*The Books of James and Peter*" pg. 163
4. "Fiery ordeal" similar to the word holocaust: William Baker - "*The Books of James and Peter*" pg. 163-164
5. We dwell on our faults, God lifts us up: William Baker - "*The Books of James and Peter*" pg. 164; NASB Study Bible pg. 1917
6. Break down unbelievers natural barriers: William Baker - "*The Books of James and Peter*" pg. 164
7. Christians should not be busybodies: William Baker - "*The Books of James and Peter*" pg. 164-165; NASB Study Bible pg. 1917; CSB Study Bible pg. 1980-1981
8. Christian character development: William Baker - "*The Books of James and Peter*" pg. 166; CSB Study Bible pg. 1981; NASB Study Bible pg. 1917
9. Outcome for unbelievers will be condemnation: William Baker - "*The Books of James and Peter*" pg. 166; NASB Study Bible pg. 1917
10. God will take care of us for doing right: William Baker - "*The Books of James and Peter*" pg. 166; ESV Study Bible pg. 2412; CSB Study Bible pg. 1981

CHAPTER 14

1. Elder amongst elders. Peter was personally there with Christ: William Baker - "*The Books of James and Peter*" pg. 167; ESV Study Bible pg. 2412; CSB Study Bible pg. 1981; NASB Study Bible pg. 1917
2. The charge of New Testament Shepherds: CSB Study Bible pg. 1981
3. *Presbuteros*: William Baker - "*The Books of James and Peter*" pg. 167
4. Peter refers to Elder(s) in the plural: NASB Study Bible pg. 1917
5. Apostles ad elders of their local church: William Baker - "*The Books of James and Peter*" pg. 167-168; NASB Study Bible pg. 1917; ESV Study Bible pg. 2412
6. Peter was an eyewitness to Christ's suffering: William Baker - "*The Books of James and Peter*" pg. 168; NASB Study Bible pg. 1917
7. Deacons and elders: William Baker - "*The Books of James and Peter*" pg. 168
8. Elders should be able to teach: NASB Study Bible pg. 1917
9. The danger of laziness: NASB Study Bible pg. 1917

10. Money should never be a motivator: William Baker - "*The Books of James and Peter*" pg. 168; NASB Study Bible pg. 1917; ESV Study Bible pg. 2412

11. Servant leadership purifies motives: William Baker - "*The Books of James and Peter*" pg. 169

12. "Lording over" forbidden by Jesus: William Baker - "*The Books of James and Peter*" pg. 169; NASB Study Bible pg. 1917-1918

13. God is bring followers to leaders: William Baker - "*The Books of James and Peter*" pg. 169

14. Jesus is the Chief Shepherd: William Baker - "*The Books of James and Peter*" pg. 169; ESV Study Bible pg. 2413; CSB Study Bible pg. 1981; NASB Study Bible pg. 1918

15. "fadeth not" term derived from the amaranth flower: NASB Study Bible pg. 1918

16. Verse 5:5 "elder" reference to age: CSB Study Bible pg. 1918;

17. Young are more headstrong and more resistant: ESV Study Bible pg. 2413

18. Lack of submission may lead to forfeiture of God's grace: William Baker - "*The Books of James and Peter*" pg. 170; CSB Study Bible pg. 1918

19. Humility allows God's will to operate through us: William Baker - "*The Books of James and Peter*" pg. 170; ESV Study Bible pg. 2413; NASB Study Bible pg. 1918

CHAPTER 15

1. God will exalt us at the right time: NASB Study Bible pg. 1918; ESV Study Bible pg. 2413; William Baker - "*The Books of James and Peter*" pg. 171

2. Stand firm in faith: NASB Study Bible pg. 1918; William Baker - "*The Books of James and Peter*" pg. 171; ESV Study Bible pg. 2413; CSB Study Bible pg. 1981

3. An incentive and reason for humility: William Baker - "*The Books of James and Peter*" pg. 171

4. God's sovereignty can be trusted: ESV Study Bible pg. 2413; William Baker - "*The Books of James and Peter*" pg. 171; NASB Study Bible pg. 1918

5. God will exalt believers in His appointed time: NASB Study Bible pg. 1918; William Baker - "*The Books of James and Peter*" pg. 171; ESV Study Bible pg. 2413

6. The return of Christ: William Baker - "*The Books of James and Peter*" pg. 171

7. "Casting" aside: Rick Renner - "*Spiritual Gems I*" pg. 324-326, 707; ESV Study Bible pg. 2413; NASB Study Bible pg. 1918

8. Can't cast aside unless someone you trust will help: William Baker - "*The Books of James and Peter*" pg. 172

9. Plan and make good choices: Rick Renner - "*Spiritual Gems I*" pg. 324-326, 707

10. Always remain alert against outside forces: ESV Study Bible pg. 2413; NASB Study Bible pg. 1918; CSB Study Bible pg. 1981

11. The devil seduces you to yield to pride: William Baker - "*The Books of James and Peter*" pg. 173

12. Be realistic about your natural tendency towards fear: ESV Study Bible pg. 2413; William Baker - "*The Books of James and Peter*" pg. 173

13. The devil is hungry to accuse: NASB Study Bible pg. 1918

14. The ability to resist implies you are living according to God's Word: NASB Study Bible pg. 1918

15. Not everyone lives the same degree of tribulation: William Baker - "*The Books of James and Peter*" pg. 173-174; NASB Study Bible pg. 1918

16. Live in away that God manifests: William Baker - "*The Books of James and Peter*" pg. 174; ESV Study Bible pg. 2413

17. Perfect you, establish you, strengthen you, and settle you: William Baker - "*The Books of James and Peter*" pg. 174; ESV Study Bible pg. 2413; NASB Study Bible pg. 1918;

18. A benediction about the ultimate goal of God: William Baker - "*The Books of James and Peter*" pg. 173

CHAPTER 16

1. Silvanus/Silas and Paul's second missionary journey: William Baker - "*The Books of James and Peter*" pg. 177; NASB Study Bible pg. 1918

2. Silvanus influence on the First Book of Peter: William Baker - "*The Books of James and Peter*" pg. 177; NASB Study Bible pg. 1918; CSB Study Bible pg. 1981

3. Christians must stand firm in the faith: William Baker - "*The Books of James and Peter*" pg. 178; ESV Study Bible pg. 2413; NASB Study Bible pg. 1918

4. Grace is the answer to how believers survive: William Baker - "*The Books of James and Peter*" pg. 178; ESV Study Bible pg. 2413; NASB Study Bible pg. 1918

5. "Babylon", city of Rome or a woman?: NASB Study Bible pg. 1918; ESV Study Bible pg. 2413; CSB Study Bible pg. 1981; William Baker - "*The Books of James and Peter*" pg. 178

6. "Mark", the Gospel of Mark and missionary journeys: NASB Study Bible pg. 1918; ESV Study Bible pg. 2413; CSB Study Bible pg. 1981; William Baker - "*The Books of James and Peter*" pg. 178

7. Modern day "church hug": William Baker - "*The Books of James and Peter*" pg. 178

Appendix: Bible Translations

When it comes to Bible translations, there are generally two competing translation schemes. One term you will notice is "formal equivalence," which more or less means a word for word translation, meaning that the word is often translated the same throughout that Bible's translation. The KJV and NASB are examples of this.

Another term you will see used is "dynamic equivalence," meaning that the translators attempted to translate the original word or phrase as closely as possible to its modern-day equivalent. The NLT is an example of this. Dynamic equivalence is not the same as a "paraphrase," such as the MSG or VOICE, but it comes close in some areas. The NIV is a translated bible that falls somewhere in between formal equivalence and dynamic equivalence.

Within this book, scripture passages are quoted from thirteen different translations and paraphrases. It is hoped that not only will you gain insight and be enlightened to truths from First Peter in this book, but that you will also have an opportunity to learn, first-hand, how different translations interpret scripture. Below is a list of the translations used, by Chapter, along with descriptions for each translation as offered by each publisher. I do not discuss pros and cons for or about each translation, instead, leaving it up to you to decide.

Chapter 3 – New American Standard Bible (NASB): The NASB does not attempt to interpret Scripture through translation. Instead, the NASB adheres to the principles of a formal equivalence translation. This is the most exacting and demanding method of translation, striving for the most readable word-for-word translation that is both accurate and clear. This method more closely follows the word and sentence patterns of the biblical authors in order to enable the reader to study Scripture in its most literal format and to experience the individual personalities of those who penned the original manuscripts.

Chapter 4 – New Living Translation (NLT): The NLT is based on the most recent scholarship in the theory of translation. The challenge for the translators was to create a text that would make the same impact in the life of modern readers that the original text had for the original readers. This is accomplished by translating entire thoughts (rather than just words) into natural, everyday English. The end result is a translation that is easy to read and understand and that accurately communicates the meaning of the original text.

Chapter 5 – Christian Standard Bible (CSB): The CSB aims to draw readers into a deeper, more meaningful relationship with God, by translating Scripture into the clearest possible modern English, allowing readers to experience God's Word at its fullest. Developed by 100 scholars from 17 denominations, the CSB faithfully and accurately captures the Bible's original meaning without compromising readability. It was created using Optimal Equivalence, a translation philosophy that balances linguistic precision to the original languages and readability in contemporary English. In the places throughout Scripture where a word-for-word rendering is clearly understandable, a literal translation is used. When a word-for-word rendering might obscure the meaning for a modern audience, a more dynamic translation is used. This process assures that both the words and thoughts contained in the original text are conveyed as accurately as possible for today's readers.

Chapter 6 – English Standard Version (ESV): The ESV is an "essentially literal" translation that seeks as far as possible to capture the precise wording of the original text and the personal style of each Bible writer. It seeks to be transparent to the original text, letting the reader see as directly as possible the structure and meaning of the original.

> The fountainhead of the ESV was William Tyndale's New Testament of 1526; marking its course were the King James Version of 1611 (KJV), the English Revised Version of 1885 (RV), the American Standard Version of 1901 (ASV), and the Revised Standard Version of 1952 and 1971 (RSV). In that stream, faithfulness to the text and vigorous pursuit of accuracy were combined with simplicity, beauty, and dignity of expression.

> To this end each word and phrase in the ESV has been carefully weighed against the original Hebrew, Aramaic, and Greek, to ensure

the fullest accuracy and clarity and to avoid under-translating or overlooking any nuance of the original text. The words and phrases themselves grow out of the Tyndale-King James legacy, and most recently out of the RSV. Archaic language has been brought to current usage and significant corrections have been made in the translation of key texts. The goal was to retain the depth of meaning and enduring language that have made their indelible mark on the English-speaking world and have defined the life and doctrine of the church over the last four centuries.

Chapter 7 – The Message (MSG): According to Eugene Peterson, the creator behind the Message [Paraphrase], it was written: "While I was teaching a class on Galatians, I began to realize that the adults in my class weren't feeling the vitality and directness that I sensed as I read and studied the New Testament in its original Greek. Writing straight from the original text, I began to attempt to bring into English the rhythms and idioms of the original language. I knew that the early readers of the New Testament were captured and engaged by these writings and I wanted my congregation to be impacted in the same way. I hoped to bring the New Testament to life for two different types of people: those who hadn't read the Bible because it seemed too distant and irrelevant and those who had read the Bible so much that it had become 'old hat.'"

Peterson's parishioners simply weren't connecting with the real meaning of the words and the relevance of the New Testament for their own lives. So he began to bring into English the rhythms and idioms of the original ancient Greek—writing straight out of the Greek text without looking at other English translations. As he shared his version of Galatians with them, they quit stirring their coffee and started catching Paul's passion and excitement as he wrote to a group of Christians whom he was guiding in the ways of Jesus Christ. For more than two years, Peterson devoted all his efforts to the New Testament in *The MSG*. His primary goal was to capture the tone of the text and the original conversational feel of the Greek, in contemporary English.

Language changes. New words are formed. Old words take on new meaning. There is a need in every generation to keep the language of the gospel message current, fresh, and understandable—the way it was for its very first readers. That is what *The Message* seeks to accomplish for contemporary readers. It is a version for our time— designed to be read by contemporary people in the same way as the original *koin* Greek and Hebrew manuscripts were savored by people thousands of years ago.

Some people like to read the Bible in Elizabethan English. Others want to read a version that gives a close word-for-word correspondence between the original languages and English. Eugene Peterson recognized that the original sentence structure is very different from that of contemporary English. He decided to strive for the spirit of the original manuscripts—to express the rhythm of the voices, the flavor of the idiomatic expressions, the subtle connotations of meaning that are often lost in English translations.

The goal of *The Message* is to engage people in the reading process and help them understand what they read. This is not a study Bible, but rather ""a reading Bible."" The verse numbers, which are not in the original documents, have been left out of the print version to facilitate easy and enjoyable reading. The original books of the Bible were not written in formal language. *The Message* tries to recapture the Word in the words we use today.

Chapter 8 – The Passion Translation (TPT): *The Passion Translation®* book of Isaiah and *New Testament with Psalms, Proverbs, and Song of Songs* is translated from Hebrew, Greek, and Aramaic texts by Dr. Brian Simmons.

The message of God's story is timeless; the Word of God doesn't change. But the methods by which that story is communicated should be timely; the vessels that steward God's Word can and should change. One of those timely methods is Bible translation. Bible translations are both a gift and a problem. They give us the words God spoke through his servants, but words can be poor containers for revelation because they leak! The meanings of words change from one generation to the next. Meaning is influenced by culture, background, and many other details. Just imagine how differently the Hebrew authors of the Old Testament saw the world three thousand years ago from the way we see it today!

There is no such thing as a truly literal translation of the Bible, for there is not an equivalent language that perfectly conveys the meaning of the biblical text. It must be understood in its original cultural and linguistic settings. This problem is best addressed when we seek to transfer meaning, not merely words, from the original text to the receptor language.

The purpose of the Passion Translation is to reintroduce the passion and fire of the Bible to the English reader. It doesn't merely convey the literal meaning of words. It expresses God's passion for people and his world by translating the original, life-changing message of God's Word for modern readers.

You will notice at times TPT italicizes certain words or phrases. These highlighted portions are not in the original Hebrew, Greek, or Aramaic manuscripts but are implied from the context. We've made these implications explicit for the sake of narrative clarity and to better convey the meaning of God's Word. This is a common practice by mainstream translations. We've also chosen to translate certain names in their original Hebrew or Greek form to better convey their cultural meaning and significance. For instance, some translations of the Bible have substituted Jacob with James and Judah with Jude. Both Greek and Aramaic leave these Hebrew names in their original form. Therefore, this translation uses those cultural names.

God longs to have his Word expressed in every language in a way that would unlock the passion of his heart. Our goal is to trigger inside every English-speaking reader an overwhelming response to the truth of the Bible. This is a heart-level translation, from the passion of God's heart to the passion of your heart.

Chapter 9 – New International Version (NIV: The NIV is a completely original translation of the Bible developed by more than one hundred scholars working from the best available Hebrew, Aramaic, and Greek texts.

An engineer working with General Electric by the name of Howard Long was a lifelong devotee of the King James Version, but when he shared it with his friends he was distressed to find that it just didn't connect. He saw the need for a translation that captured the truths he loved in the language that his contemporaries spoke.

For 10 years, Long and a growing group of like-minded supporters drove this idea. The passion of one man became the passion of a

church, and ultimately the passion of a whole group of
denominations. And finally, in 1965, after several years of
preparatory study, a trans-denominational group of scholars agreed
to begin work on the project – determining to not simply adapt an
existing English version of the Bible but to start from scratch with
the best available manuscripts in the original languages. Their
conclusion was endorsed by a large number of church leaders who
met in Chicago in 1966.

A self-governing body of fifteen biblical scholars, the Committee on
Bible Translation (CBT) was formed and charged with responsibility
for the version, and in 1968 the New York Bible Society (which
subsequently became the International Bible Society and then
Biblica) undertook the financial sponsorship of the project. The
translation of each book was assigned to translation teams, each
made up of two lead translators, two translation consultants, and a
stylistic consultant where necessary. The initial translations
produced by these teams were carefully scrutinized and revised by
intermediate editorial committees of five biblical scholars to check
them against the source texts and assess them for
comprehensibility. Each edited text was then submitted to a general
committee of eight to twelve members before being distributed to
selected outside critics and to all members of the CBT in
preparation for a final review. Samples of the translation were
tested for clarity and ease of reading with pastors, students,
scholars, and lay people across the full breadth of the intended
audience. Perhaps no other translation has undergone a more
thorough process of review and revision. From the very start, the
NIV sought to bring modern Bible readers as close as possible to the
experience of the very first Bible readers: providing the best
possible blend of transparency to the original documents and
comprehension of the original meaning in every verse. With this
clarity of focus, however, came the realization that the work of
translating the NIV would never be truly complete. As new
discoveries were made about the biblical world and its languages,
and as the norms of English usage developed and changed over
time, the NIV would also need to change to hold true to its original
vision.

Chapter 10 – New English Translation (NET): The NET Bible is a
completely new translation of the Bible, not a revision or an update of a
previous English version. It was completed by more than 25 biblical

scholars—experts in the original biblical languages—who worked directly from the best currently available Hebrew, Aramaic, and Greek texts.

Most of these scholars teach Old or New Testament exegesis in seminaries and graduate schools. Furthermore, the translator assigned to prepare the first draft of the translation and notes for each book of the Bible was chosen in every instance because of his or her extensive work in that particular book—not only involving teaching but writing and research as well, often extending over several decades. Many of the translators and editors have also participated in other translation projects. They have been assisted by doctoral students and advised by style consultants and Wycliffe field translators. Hence, the notes alone are the cumulative result of hundreds of thousands of hours of biblical and linguistic research applied to the particular problems of accurately translating and interpreting the text. The translators' notes, most of which were created at the same time as the initial drafts of the translation itself, enable the reader of the NET Bible to "look over the shoulders" of the translators as they worked and gain insight into their decisions and choices to an extent never before possible in an English translation.

One of the goals of the NET Bible with the complete set of translators' notes is to allow the general public—as well as Bible students, pastors, missionaries, and Bible translators in the field—to be able to know what the translators of the NET Bible were thinking when a phrase or verse was rendered in a particular way. Many times the translator will have made informed decisions based on facts about grammatical, lexical, historical, and textual data not readily available to English-speaking students of the Bible. This information is now easily accessible through the translators' notes.

Chapter 11 – New Century Version (NCV): The NCV is an English translation of the Bible with roots extending to the English Version for the Deaf (EVD) Bible translation (by the World Bible Translation Center, a subsidiary of Bible League International). It is also related to the Easy-to-Read Version (ERV), having longer sentences and a more fluent style.

The translation team of 50 Bible scholars and translators included people with translation experience on such versions as the NIV, the NASB, and the NKJV. The best available Hebrew and Greek texts were used, principally the third edition of the United Bible Societies'

Greek text and the latest edition of the Biblia Hebraica, along with the Septuagint.

Chapter 12 – The Voice (VOICE): *The Voice* was created for and by a church in great transition. Throughout the body of Christ, extensive discussions are ongoing about a variety of issues including which style of worship is most appropriate, how we distinguish cultural expressions from genuine expressions of faith, what it means to live the gospel, and how we faithfully communicate the essential truths of historic Christianity. At the center of these discussions is the role of Scripture. Instead of widening the division between culture and theology, it is time to bring the body of Christ together again around the Bible.

Most English translations attempt to even out the literary styles of the different scripture authors in sentence structure and vocabulary. Instead, **The Voice** distinguishes the unique perspective of each author, retelling the story of the Bible in a form as fluid as modern literary works while remaining painstakingly true to the original Greek, Hebrew, and Aramaic texts. Accomplished writers and biblical scholars teamed up to create an English rendering that, while of great artistic value, is carefully aligned with the meaning inherent in the original language. Attention is paid to the use of idioms, artistic elements, confusion of pronouns, repetition of conjunctions, modern sentence structure, and the public reading of the passage.

Chapter 13 – New American Standard Bible (NASB): See Chapter 3 description

Chapter 14 – King James Version (KJV): In 1604, King James I of England authorized that a new translation of the Bible into English be started. It was finished in 1611, just 85 years after the first translation of the New Testament into English appeared (Tyndale, 1526). The Authorized Version, or King James Version, quickly became the standard for English-speaking Protestants. Its flowing language and prose rhythm has had a profound influence on the literature of the past 400 years. The King James Version present on the Bible Gateway matches the 1987 printing. The KJV is public domain in the United States.

Chapter 15 – New King James Version (NKJV): Commissioned in 1975 by Thomas Nelson Publishers, 130 respected Bible scholars, church leaders, and lay Christians worked for seven years to create a completely new, modern translation of Scripture, yet one that would retain the purity and stylistic beauty of the original King James. With unyielding faithfulness to the original Greek, Hebrew, and Aramaic texts, the translation applies the most recent research in archaeology, linguistics, and textual studies.

Chapter 16 – Amplified Bible (AMP): The Amplified Bible of 2015 includes more amplification in the Old Testament and refined amplification in the New Testament. Additionally, the Bible text has been improved to read smoothly with or without amplifications, so that the text may be read either way. The same feel and style of amplification has been maintained, so that those who read the classic Amplified Bible will be able to easily transition to the new text.

The AMP was the first Bible project of The Lockman Foundation. Its goal was to take both word meaning and context into account to accurately translate the original text from one language into another. The AMP does this through the use of explanatory alternate readings and amplifications to assist the reader in understanding what Scripture really says. Multiple English word equivalents to each key Hebrew and Greek word clarify and amplify meanings that may otherwise have been concealed by the traditional translation method. The first edition was published in 1965.

The AMP is based on the American Standard Version of 1901, Rudolph Kittel's Biblia Hebraica, the Greek text of Westcott and Hort, and the 23rd edition of the Nestle Greek New Testament as well as the best Hebrew and Greek lexicons available at the time. Cognate languages, the Dead Sea Scrolls, and other Greek works were also consulted. The Septuagint and other versions were compared for interpretation of textual differences. In completing the Amplified Bible, translators made a determined effort to keep, as far as possible, the familiar wording of the earlier versions, and especially the feeling of the ancient Book.

Bibliography

Baker, William (2004). The Books of James & Peter, First and Second: Faith, Suffering, and Knowledge, AMG Publishers.

Kistermaker, Simon J. (1987). Peter and Jude, Baker Publishing Group.

Luther, Martin (2005). Commentary on Peter and Jude, Kregel Classics.

Renner, Rick (2003). Sparkling Gems Volume I, Harrison House Publishers.

Renner, Rick (2016). Sparkling Gems Volume II, Harrison House Publishers.

Schreiner, Thomas R. (2008). New Testament Theology: Magnifying God in Christ, Baker Academic.

Christian Standard Bible (CSB) Study Bible (2017), Holman Bible Publishers.

English Standard Version (ESV) Study Bible (2008), Crossway.

New American Standard Bible (NASB), The MacArthur Study Bible (2006), Thomas Nelson.

https://en.wikipedia.org/wiki/Saint_Peter, accessed Feb 2021

https://overviewbible.com/apostle-peter/, accessed Feb 2021

https://en.wikipedia.org/wiki/Reprobation, accessed March 2021

https://en.wikipedia.org/wiki/Predestination, accessed March 2021

Contact

Marcus can be reached:

https://thewildernessprojectexperience.com/

Email: fhghministries@gmail.com

About the Author

Marcus is a military veteran, retiring from the US Army after 20 years of service as both an enlisted soldier and commissioned officer. After his retirement, he served in multiple senior executive positions in both the private and public sectors. Marcus answered the call to the Lord when he was almost 40 years old, prior to which he lived his life wandering lost with no hope.

Marcus left Corporate America in 2019 and founded FHGH Ministries with his wife of 32 years, Julee. He and Julee are the parents of two sons and a daughter, one of whom died in 2011 while serving in the Air Force in the country of Qatar.

Marcus has a Doctorate in IT Leadership (ABD) and a Doctor of Ministry. He is known for being honest and transparent about the struggles and challenges of life, but he also believes that it is the lies men tell themselves, and each other, every day that are killing them. However, he also knows that it is the love, grace, and mercy of our Lord Jesus Christ that is the HOPE for all – our source of Joy and Peace in the world today.

Marcus is currently the author of three books, one of which won an International Award in 2020, and regularly writes articles for Christian magazines and blog sites.